THE
ADDICTION
BATTLE

Three Tools to End It Now

Timothy J. Wulff, L.M.S.W.

Addicus Books
Omaha, Nebraska

An Addicus Nonfiction Book

ISBN: 978-1-950091-27-0
Typography and cover by Jack Kusler

This book is not intended to be a substitute for a physician, nor does the author intend to give advice contrary to that of an attending physician.

Library of Congress Cataloging-in-Publication Data
Names: Wulff, Timothy J., author.
Title: The addiction battle : three tools to end it now / Timothy J. Wulff.
Description: First Edition. | Omaha : Addicus Books, Inc., 2020. | Includes index.
Identifiers: LCCN 2020027153 (print) | LCCN 2020027154 (ebook) | ISBN 9781950091270 (trade paperback) | ISBN 9781950091447 (pdf) | ISBN 9781950091454 (epub) | ISBN 9781950091461 (kindle edition)
Subjects: LCSH: Substance abuse—Psychological aspects. Substance abuse—Treatment. | Addicts—Psychology. | Addicts—Rehabilitation.
Classification: LCC HV4998 .W85 2020 (print) | LCC HV4998 (ebook) | DDC 616.86/06—dc23
LC record available at https://lccn.loc.gov/2020027153
LC ebook record available at https://lccn.loc.gov/2020027154

Addicus Books, Inc.
P.O. Box 45327
Omaha, Nebraska 68145
AddicusBooks.com
Printed in the United States of America
10 9 8 7 6 5 4 3 2 1

To my wife, Dr. Kara Jo Hoisington Wulff. There is no dream I have that is too big for you to support. Thank you for your encouragement, patience, and unwavering love. I love you.

To my children, Grayson and Gabriella. You are the greatest gifts I have ever been given. Both of you inspire me to live a life in pursuit of dreams. Don't ever let anyone tell you that you cannot follow yours. I love you more than you could ever imagine.

To my friend and mentor, Nick Frankforter. This book would not exist without your ongoing patience, teaching, mentorship, and friendship. I hope this book does as much for those reading it as you did for me.

Strength does not come from winning. Your struggles develop your strengths. When you go through hardships and decide not to surrender, that is strength.

—Arnold Schwarzenegger

Contents

Acknowledgments

I would like to express my gratitude to those who have supported me and helped to make this book a reality. To God my heavenly Father. Everything I am or I have is because You allowed it to be. Separated from You, I am nothing.

To my earthly father, Dr. Jonathan Wulff. You are virtuous. You consistently model faith, commitment, discipline, hard work, integrity, wisdom, and strength. It is infectious, and I thank you for all that you are and all that you do.

To my mother, Cyndy Wulff. There is no doubt I absorbed your creativity and caring heart. Without either of these qualities, the fire in my belly would most certainly burn out.

To my big brother, Mark Wulff. You have been my best friend, my buddy, my teacher, my coach, my biggest cheerleader, and my hero. For this, and the countless other roles you have played in my life, thank you.

To my sister, Michelle Gallo. When you have a million things to do, if I need you, you will marvelously make time for a million and one. Thank you for your continued support.

To my baby brother, Dr. Steven Wulff. It's not always the big brother who is to be looked up to. You model so many qualities that inspire me to be a better person.

I wish to acknowledge my in-laws, Dr. David and Kathi Hoisington. To all my newest siblings, Jeff Gallo, Heather Wulff, Elisha Wulff, Karlynn Blahnik, David Blahnik, Brant Hoisington.

To my nieces and nephews, Lorelai, Xander, Janae, Merrick, Sophie, Ethan, Brek, and Koen. Always, always follow your dreams.

Thank you my best friends, Karl Wyble, Dr. Chris Sherry, Troy Huddelson, Brian Stuitje, Corey Doll, Jay Graves, Grant Pierce, Jason Cornelius.

To Rod Colvin and Addicus Books. You took a chance on me, taught me, guided me, supported me, and challenged me. Thank you for helping to make this dream a reality. To my editor, Susan Adams. You are simply amazing. Thank you for your friendship, guidance, and pushing me further than I thought I could go.

To my mentors, Nick Frankforter, Dr. Samantha Wheeler, Dr. Kathy Bailey, Dr, Steve Geiger, Steve Cottrell. To my work family at Comprehensive Psychological Services, with a special thanks to Dr. Jon Shy, Dr. Steve Geiger, Kim Podmore, Randi Baker.

I wish to remember those who are no longer with us: Dorothy Gall, Rev. Arnold and Ruth Wulff, and Nikki Wyble.

Lastly, I acknowledge my countless clients who have shared their stories and trusted me with their care.

Introduction

If you've been struggling with addiction, you already know the negative emotional, spiritual, and mental pain it causes. You also know about the damage addiction causes to relationships with loved ones. I would like to help you bring an end to the pain that addiction has caused you.

I wrote this book to teach you a new way to end your addiction. I have spent over a decade perfecting this approach. It's simple and effective. And, I have witnessed firsthand how this approach has helped many of my clients understand themselves and their addiction. I have seen the light in their eyes, the "ah-ha" moment, when these concepts begin to make sense to them. I want you to experience this, too. I want you to understand why you fell into the addiction trap, and I want you to feel the hope that my clients feel when they understand what it takes to overcome their addiction.

If you are a substance user and want to stop, this book is for you! I am going to provide you with tools that teach you why you were pulled into addictive behavior in the first place. You will learn how your true-self was damaged and how it can recover. Moreover, I will teach you the three most essential characteristics of the true-self that will help you recover from addiction.

Here is the best part: You already have these powerful tools! You just don't know it yet!

—*Timothy Wulff, L.M.S.W.*

Part I

The Addiction Blueprint: Accommodation

1

A New Approach to
Treating Addiction

The important thing is not to stop questioning.
—Albert Einstein

Her name was Danielle. She came to my office seeking therapy for help battling a lifelong struggle with addiction. I could tell she was frail as I walked her the nearly twenty feet from our reception desk to my office. Danielle reported feeling frustrated and exhausted. Although she was only twenty-nine years old, the wrinkled skin on her face and lifeless look in her eyes made her appear much older. Her clothes, dirty and mismatched, seemed to hang on her frail body.

Danielle's life had been a series of superficial thrills, chasing whatever felt good in the moment. As a child she was curious, as a teen devious, now as an adult she was hopeless like many others who feel they will never escape the grips of addiction.

Although she admitted to years of sporadic psychotherapy and participating in numerous self-help groups, Danielle had grown tired of the same advice. Her family challenged her will power and questioned her morality. Her doctors referred to her as sick, her friends labeled her as immature, and her self-help group told her she had flawed thinking. By the time Danielle arrived at my office, she was better educated on flawed thinking, behavioral modification, and the twelve steps of Alcoholics Anonymous than I was.

However, Danielle's inability to correct her thinking and control behavioral impulses left her questioning the same things her loved ones did. Was she just weak? Immature? Immoral? Behind her sunken tired eyes, I saw desperation. I looked at this young woman sitting across from me and asked her if she was willing to do anything different this time in therapy. Danielle responded with two words: "Whatcha got?"

I knew what Danielle meant with her mildly snarky question. She was searching for something, *anything* that would help her understand more about why she was addicted. Danielle had become tired of the same approaches to treatment, yet managed to remain open to the possibility I could provide her something new or different.

Indeed, I did have something new to share with Danielle, and now I want to share it with you. I want to teach you how your addictive tendencies likely developed long before you ever picked up a drug or alcoholic drink. Moreover, I want to give you tools for stopping your addiction now.

Understanding the Addiction Trap

Are you with me? Are you ready to learn how your addictive personality developed and what you can do about it now? I truly hope so. Before we get into the actual tools and skills you will undoubtedly need, it's important for me to tell you a little about where I came from and how I, too, became frustrated with some of the current therapeutic methods to treat addiction.

Early on, I learned the dangers of drugs in elementary school while participating in the D.A.R.E. program. If you are not familiar with D.A.R.E., it stands for Drug Abuse Resistance Education, which in my town was provided by the local police department. Our elementary school had a police officer, Officer Friendly, who came to our class on occasion to teach us about drug use and abuse. These meetings were fun and almost everyone knew and liked Officer Friendly.

My fellow classmates and I all had the same education, during the same phase of life, with Officer Friendly. Moreover, in elementary school, everyone seemed to buy into the notion that drugs were bad and something to avoid. However, as the years passed, many of us would go on to experiment with the same dangerous chemicals (alcohol, tobacco, marijuana, LSD, cocaine, opioids). These are chemicals that terrified us at one point in our lives. Sadly, some of us would develop severe drug and alcohol dependencies.

So why then did some of us choose abstinence or just experimentation, while others got caught in the web of addiction and dependency? The answer, of course, is that education is not nearly enough. We have the facts, know the statistics, rationally see the consequences, yet we indulge. When it comes to addiction, whether it's chemical abuse, alcohol addiction, shopping addiction, sex addiction, food addiction, or chronic gambling, we know the consequences. Yet it doesn't stop us.

After witnessing how addiction had changed my peers, some being my best friends, I was determined to try to be part of some kind of solution. Originally, I wanted to become a policeman and work in the D.A.R.E. program just as Officer Friendly had. However, the more I began to realize that education is not the answer, I knew I needed to find a career that would more appropriately help me reach my goal.

I knew there was no guaranteed method to determine who will develop addiction through experimentation and who will not. What I did know was that for those who develop addictive disorders, more education on the negative effects of the behavior is not the answer. I wanted to move beyond lecturing consequences and seek to understand what drives the addictive behavior in the first place. In doing so, I knew the problem could stop before it begins. So I became a therapist.

Understanding the Roots of Addiction

I worked hard to try to discover the actual root cause of addiction. I figured if I knew that, I could help people stop the problem before it starts. While in graduate school, I learned about primitive and extreme methods to treat addiction. In years past, these methods included exorcisms, sterilizations, and shock therapy. Sometimes, even lobotomies were performed, which is a crude surgery performed on the front of the brain to "cure" mental illness. Other theories included the use of psychedelics and hallucinogens as treatment for addiction.

I was lucky enough to get a yearlong internship in the addiction unit at a local hospital where I was exposed to many traditional and widely practiced methods to treat addiction. I witnessed detoxification with medications such as benzodiazepines, Campral, and naltrexone, among others. When the patients in the unit eventually detoxed, they were given educational treatment as well as counseling.

Many of the behavioral therapies focused on modifying attitudes and behaviors related to drug use. Other therapies such as cognitive-behavioral therapy (CBT), helped clients use rational thinking to recognize and avoid triggers, as well as cope with situations in which they were most likely to use. Often, family members were invited in to discuss relapse prevention and develop a plan for the patient to return home.

All of the patients in these therapies were required to participate in Alcoholics Anonymous or Narcotics Anonymous. Family members were encouraged to participate in Al-Anon, a support group for families and others who have a chemically addicted loved one. Around the same time, there was a push for counselors to learn skills in motivational interviewing as a method to elicit

"change talk," which was intended to guide clients in coming up with their own compelling reasons to change their behavior. Yet with all of the help and support of these types of therapies, relapse remained a problem.

Even though the hospital where I was interning provided excellent care with quality professionals, I would see the same clients return to the detox unit after relapse. I couldn't help continuing to ask myself if there was something missing. To me, behavior change and education still seemed to be only a piece of a bigger picture. What was the missing piece? This question only fueled my desire to want to find the answer. What's more, the clients I worked with were only a tiny fraction of those impacted by addiction.

According to the Substance Abuse and Mental Health Services Administration (SAMHSA), in 2018, nearly 53,182 people age twelve and older reportedly used illicit drugs within the past year. An astonishing 31,918 of those had used in the past month. The National Institute on Drug Abuse (NIDA) estimates drug addiction costs our nation more than $740 billion annually in health care, drug-related crime, and lost work productivity. These are just the numbers we are aware of and do not account for those people or instances never reported. Moreover, these statistics do not consider the health-related costs resulting from food addiction as millions of people are chronically addicted to refined flour and sugar.

We have more and easier access to addictive chemicals than ever before. The old street corner drug dealer now competes with the Internet and schools where students sell or share the narcotics they find in their medicine cabinets at home. Newer synthetic drugs are being manufactured all the time, even being branded as "safe alternatives." Fast food, junk food, and sugar drinks are cheap, legal, convenient, and available.

Our society is slowly growing desensitized to the real dangers of all addictive chemicals as we see legalization and decriminalization of marijuana and Hollywood romanticizing drug and alcohol use. A multi-billion-dollar pharmaceutical industry spends millions on television advertisements in attempts to convince viewers which chemicals they "need." Not many people deny there is a growing problem. Those who do aren't paying very close attention to what is going on around them. These problems are real and affect not only the individual who is addicted, but also their loved ones and society as a whole.

I am very proud to say I have worked hard to earn the credentials that allow me to work in the field of psychotherapy with those who are addicted. In nearly a decade of conducting therapy with clients who have various problems, I have come to believe addiction seems to be the most misunderstood—not only misunderstood by my clients but by much of society.

Although advances in technology and medicine continue to enhance treatment options, the underlying cause of addiction is ambiguous at best. Science has discovered through research that there is a genetic component to addiction. Many of those studies have found that over 50 percent of alcohol-related disorders may be hereditary. Although fewer studies have focused on illicit drug use, there is still evidence of a strong hereditary connection.

Many self-help programs continue to assist with the behavioral and social component of addiction, that is, a focus on changing specific behaviors such as avoiding events, people, and places that trigger you to use. However, as much as we know about addiction, we still do not know much at all. We have only educated guesses as to why one person can stop a behavior before they become addicted while another may engage in a behavior and never stop until they suffer catastrophic consequences.

It's time for you to learn what truly causes your tendency to dive into the cycle of addiction. It's time for you to learn how to use what you already have within you to get your life back. So, welcome to an exciting journey.

It is because of this uncertainty that treatment for addiction has become a practice rather than an exact science. Many practitioners are using treatment methods focused on abstinence and relapse prevention, support groups, cognitive behavioral therapy, and medication.

Although these treatment methods all have merit, they do little to address the actual cause of the addiction. This is because we simply do not know for certain what the cause of addiction is. Nevertheless, these "Band-Aid" approaches leave people with methods on how to deal with the symptoms of the addiction rather than attack the cause of addiction.

This leaves people like Danielle asking what else ya got. What I will teach you in this book is exactly what I spent months teaching her and many like her. Using the tools I provided her, she was not only able to get sober, but also to have a highly satisfying, stable career and significantly improved personal relationships.

7

If you are struggling with addiction, there is a chance you have been exposed to some of the treatment methods I discussed earlier. However, maybe you do not necessarily agree with how doctors, therapists, books, or loved ones view the problems you are facing. Or maybe you, like me, feel there is something missing.

When I am working with a client, I am always curious about how they view their addiction. In the past decade, I have heard everything from "I have a disease" and "I have no will power" to "I'm very weak," "I'm broken," or even "I'm evil." Perhaps you have looked at yourself in one or more of these ways.

Maybe a support group or loved ones have also used these harsh statements to describe you or addiction. Maybe you are like my client Danielle and wonder if there are other methods to help address the problem you are facing. Or perhaps you are tired of the same treatments that feel helpful in the short term but have not taught you the actual root cause of your addiction. I am going to help you learn how to use tools you already have to change your life. First, I want to introduce some core concepts that will be absolutely imperative in your journey to health and sobriety.

The Basic Tools:
Anger, Selfishness, and Troublemaking

There are three core concepts to the approach I will teach you. These concepts, when redefined and used appropriately, will help you free yourself from your addictive cycle. Since I have a chapter dedicated to each of these concepts, I will mention them only briefly here.

Anger

I will challenge how you think about anger. I will make an argument that anger, appropriately expressed, is not only a good thing, but essential for recovery. I will be discussing the purpose of anger as well as how proper access to your anger will firmly aid you in sobriety.

Selfishness

By selfishness I am referring to healthy selfishness or self-care. In chapter 5, I will teach you the difference between healthy selfishness and unhealthy selfishness. Furthermore, I will help you understand how healthy selfishness is a necessary component of sobriety.

Troublemaking

I will challenge the notion that making trouble is unhealthy by instructing you how to make "trouble" appropriately.

You will learn that all of these often-misunderstood concepts are enormous assets for you. It's time for you to learn what truly causes your tendency to dive into the cycle of addiction. It's time for you to learn how to use what you already have within you to get your life back.

So, welcome to an exciting journey. I am pleased to present to you an alternative approach, one that will change your life. I warn you though that this approach, although simple, is not easy. It involves first exploring and understanding your earliest relational experiences. You will find how these early relational dynamics have been the blueprint for the development of addictive tendencies. By "relational dynamics," I am referring to our relationship style and patterns—how we behave, relate, and interact in our personal relationships.

It may be painful to learn that, often, families, friends, society, and even some forms of addiction treatments are mirroring the very dynamic of these relationships, thus perpetuating the problem. This point of view will not be taken lightly by many people in the addiction community. Some may even be bothered by some of my strong opinions on this subject.

Although I firmly believe my treatment method can stand on its own, many of my clients are working on these skills in addition to working with self-help programs. However, many of them are sustaining sobriety by following my approach only. That is not to say emotional support is unnecessary. My approach is not about eliminating support, but rather recruiting the right kind of support to be successful. Much like anything else in life, you will get out of it what you put in. It has been my experience that when people work hard to challenge themselves with this approach, they are able to achieve and sustain sobriety.

Summary

Addiction is complicated and destructive. It can have massive consequences for an individual, family, and society. Although our knowledge on how to treat addiction continues to improve, there are many people who are still searching for more answers. Like me, and Danielle, there is hope that a different perspective on addiction treatment can finally clarify what is necessary to stay sober once and for all.

2

The Caretaker

Some people will hurt you and then
act like you hurt them.

—Unknown

Many of my clients who come to treatment for the first time know nothing about therapy other than what they've heard from others or have seen in the media. It is not uncommon for them to ask, "Should I lay down and complain about my mom?" Although this is often the stereotypical image portrayed in fictional stories, it is true that quality therapy must address our early life experiences. The reason is that all of us are shaped by our earliest relationship experiences. Moreover, in these early relationships, almost everyone has become an accommodator to some degree. Put simply, we learn early on how to take care of others.

In this chapter you will learn how relationships have taught you to become a caretaker. Although early relationships begin at home, influences outside the home can easily strengthen your "need" to be a caretaker for others or to overly accommodate them. Let's take a look at what's at stake when you accommodate others too much.

Accommodating Others

When we learn to overly accommodate others, it will hinder the growth of our authentic, true-self. Our true and authentic self consists of all of our limitless potential, profound feelings, sweet desires, and powerful urges. Limiting the true-self will keep us from developing in ways that are necessary to ensure we are emotionally healthy and safe.

Our true and authentic self consists of all of our limitless potential, profound feelings, sweet desires, and powerful urges. Limiting the true-self will keep us from developing in ways that are necessary to ensure we are emotionally healthy and safe.

We simply do not live in a world that is always safe, comforting, and accepting. There are multiple influences, varying in importance and intensity, giving us constant feedback on how we should behave, think, or live our lives. Any deviation from family, school, employment, or societal expectations is often met with judgment, criticism, confusion, or concern from those who are setting our "rules."

Surely, we need rules, norms, expectations, and standards in order to ensure a functioning society. However, many of these expectations and standards can go far beyond what is necessary and therefore stunt the development of an individual. What is necessary is consistent effort to acknowledge the uniqueness of an individual. This includes all desires, dreams, feelings, and urges, even if they do not match those of the caretakers, teachers, and others. From what I have observed, this is often not happening. And it is a great tragedy, one that I see daily in my clinical practice.

Unlike other problems my clients have, loss of their true-self is often something they do not even realize has happened. I am not referring to an adolescent or adult expressing their individuality through behavior or physical presentation. The tragedy is the loss of the child inside of us that was neglected or abused during our earliest years. This damage begins with our early caretakers but is often repeated through relationships outside our families. So what is involved in "healthy" relational dynamics?

A Child's Emotional Development

In an ideal family setting, a newborn child becomes a center of attention. Hopefully, the child's every feeling, urge, dream, desire, and need is tended to by the earliest caregivers. The child is given the freedom to explore their own true-self, experience a spectrum of emotions, be assertive with their needs, and feel the power of desire. When the child is given this freedom, the burden of the sacrifice then becomes the caregivers to bear.

As the child grows, makes mistakes, learns likes and dislikes, discovers dreams, and explores personal power, hopefully the family unit would fully support and help foster this independence. The child would not hesitate to state an opinion, express an emotion, or explore personal interests. In fact, all of these endeavors would be encouraged and supported. Not one part of the child's sense of security would be threatened by being true to who they are. Secure children, and adults, feel confident to be spontaneous with their true-self. In other words, they feel safe.

In an ideal world, not just parents and early care-takers, but other authority figures, peers, and colleagues would demonstrate keen interest in fostering the growth of the child's true-self. In this ideal scenario, socialization is still a healthy expectation. Just because a child has their true-self honored and validated, it does not mean they get everything they desire. For example, I can empathize and honor my five-year-old daughter's desire to eat a gallon of ice cream before dinner while not allowing it to happen. Honoring the true-self simply means a person can safely own all the elements of their true-self and receive encouragement, love, and support from those around them.

Growing Up in an Imperfect World

However, we obviously do not live in a perfect or ideal world. Our parents and caretakers make mistakes, and the world can be cruel. We live in a world full of expectations. Even while the child is in utero, parents make bold predictions for their future NFL superstar or neurosurgeon. Well-intended parents will continue to project their expectations and hopes as they plan for room decorations, toys, colors, books, even the "best" day care centers. It's almost as if the child is born with a job to live up to those expectations.

Honoring the true-self simply means a person can safely own all the elements of their true-self and receive encouragement, love, and support from those around them.

As the child grows and begins to communicate, parents learn their child's interests, how they express feelings, their likes and dislikes. What if they don't match what the parents want? What if the son who was expected to be a brilliant physician has no natural aptitude for medical science? What if the daughter who was supposed to be the athlete hates sports? The result is often rejection.

The manner or magnitude of the rejection may be subtle, such as a parent's shift from joy to sadness as they learn their child doesn't have their same interests. Children will intuitively observe this shift in demeanor and will be impacted, even though the child may not be consciously aware of it. Think about your own history. How does it feel to disappoint a loved one? Did someone really have to tell you they were disappointed or did you often just know based on nonverbal cues? Even as an adult, with a much more mature understanding of life, it can feel awful to disappoint. Imagine disappointing someone just by being who you are, having certain feelings, or specific dreams and desires.

I hear these subtle rejections all the time when parents express their disappointments about their child with statements such as, "she never slept through the night," "she was late walking," "he won't play ball with me," "I don't like his friends," "something is wrong with her—she dyed her hair blue." Children hear such disappointment as rejection. Even when the comments express mere concern, the child's underdeveloped brain is not capable of deciphering the difference between mild parental concern and rejection.

Why do parents and other caretakers feel disappointment? Because they all had expectations about their child's development, education, peer group, school performance, appearance, and interests. As I stated, I believe not living up to others' expectations are rejections.

Steve's Story

I once worked with a client whom I will call Steve. He was fifty-eight years old and himself a therapist. Steve would often talk about how his father indirectly rejected his son's true-self and desire. During one of our sessions he said, "My mother would basically force my dad to spend quality time with me. But we never did what I wanted. To my dad, quality time involved taking me out with him during an activity he wanted to do. Any time I would suggest something different, he would say, maybe next time." Even though Steve never experienced any emotional or physical abuse and was otherwise well taken care of, he felt rejected by the one person he wanted to be accepted by the most. This was mostly due to his father's unwillingness to explore and honor Steve's unique wants and desires. Rather, the dad honored his own desires and took his son along for the ride.

Many children grow up in families with overt rejection, neglect, and abuse. The expectations in these families are that children be quiet, behave, and comply with whatever the caregiver wants. In these environments, there is no parental sacrifice, no nurturing, and no safety. The children's true-self is not honored. Rather than caring for their children first, some parents and caretakers fulfill their own needs, desires, and urges. In some cases, these children are even abused physically or sexually.

As children instinctively know, their survival is dependent on their caretakers. So what happens to the child's unique, true, authentic self? As a survival mechanism, the child's true-self goes underground and into the unconscious of his or her psyche. The child is essentially hiding his or her true-self to accommodate and please caretakers. If this continues long enough, the true-self will be hidden from everyone, including the child's inner self. The result is a lack of self-esteem or self-identity, impaired ability to express feelings, and difficulty building and maintaining healthy boundaries. I will explore boundaries in more detail in chapter 4. Put simply, boundaries refer to keeping a healthy distance between you and whatever can cause you harm.

Neglecting parts of ourselves to please or care for others does not happen only in childhood, or only as a result of abuse or neglect. Major traumas such as the loss of a parent can result in a child unconsciously suppressing elements of themselves in an attempt to avoid causing any additional stress within the family. In adulthood, a person may suppress characteristics of themselves in an attempt to "help" loved ones.

Sara's Story

I once worked with a woman whom I will call Sara. She was extremely intelligent and at one time had political aspirations. Sara had met and married her husband while still in college. Both excelled in academics and

16

had lofty career goals, she in politics and he in medicine. After graduating from college, Sara decided to let her husband follow his dream of becoming a physician. For eight years, Sara supported her husband's every move from medical school to residency, and then through his fellowship. All the while, Sara put her own dreams on hold. However, when Sara's husband completed his schooling and training and it was her time, she was surprised to discover she was pregnant.

Sara spent the next eighteen years raising her three children, never realizing her own career goals. Her time was filled with scheduling children's activities, serving on school boards, and handling household responsibilities. After her children graduated from high school, Sara tried to focus back on herself but realized she had completely lost touch with that young, assertive, goal-driven woman of the past. She felt depressed, alone, and completely lost. Sara began drinking to ease the pain and try to escape the loneliness. By the time she came to see me, Sara was a full-blown alcoholic.

During the course of therapy, Sara learned how to incorporate the elements into her life that I am going to teach you. Although she had a brief relapse, Sara managed to use the skills I taught her to remain sober. Moreover, her new skill set resulted in healthier relationships with her husband, children, and, eventually, grandchildren.

As people lock away aspects of their true-self to accommodate others, their unique qualities become buried deep in their unconscious minds. The skills I taught Sara and will teach you involve understanding and using aspects of your true-self to end your addiction. As I mentioned earlier, I am talking primarily about anger, healthy selfishness, and troublemaking. I understand these qualities are not commonly thought of as being good. Most parents are not usually proud to say their children are angry, selfish, or troublemakers. Moreover, we live in a society that can demonize these qualities as well.

If you take a moment to think about it, when is the last time you heard any of these qualities discussed in a way that is not negative? It is likely you never have. However, I have come to believe our negative perspectives on these characteristics are misdirected and inappropriate. I want you to understand how you define anger, selfishness, and troublemaking will make an enormous difference.

The Shadow Version of Self

Every emotion has what I call a "shadow" version of itself. The shadow version is a destructive or clumsy display of an otherwise healthy and necessary component of the true-self. When someone is overwhelmed by a shadow manifestation, they often experience it without owning it as part of them or have a "that's not me" moment. They may feel as if experiencing the emotion or behavior happened because they were "taken over" by something that is otherwise not a part of them. I have worked with many clients who have impulsive anger outbursts. Many of these men and women are otherwise kind and giving with pleasant dispositions. When they discuss their anger outbursts it is not uncommon for me to hear, "the crazy thing is, I'm not normally an angry person." This is because their anger has been suppressed into their shadow rather than incorporated into their ego. This kind of statement reflects the shadow self.

Although it may be true that they are "taken over," it is not from some outside force, but rather from what is very much a part of them. They just don't see it that way. Some of our biggest problems arise by pretending we don't have feelings, urges, or desires. The truth is, we all experience anger, sadness, embarrassment, joy, and fear. Everyone has dreams, urges, and desires. It is only when we refuse to acknowledge them that they permeate deep in the psyche's shadow. When these characteristics emerge from the depths of the shadow, we often do not like to face them.

This sudden emergence of intense emotion happens primarily because our psyche is out of balance. Emotion is energy and energy cannot disappear, it can only be moved. If you were to deny or hide a particular emotion you are having, it doesn't just go away. The saying "time heals all wounds" is inaccurate. Your emotion is energy and it will remain with you. If you do not express emotion appropriately, your psyche will hang on to the energy that was designed to move through you. The weight of holding onto this energy will create an imbalance as it will be stored up internally.

Dealing with Buried Feelings

If you do not consciously acknowledge and own the various elements of your true-self, you will be weighed down by stored-up energy. Ever felt exhausted because you were at a job or entertaining guests and had to put on a smile even though you were anything but happy? It is exhausting because you are hiding your true feelings and putting up a facade. When we do this, our psyche wants relief from the inner conflict. However, often we don't make a conscious effort to honor those true feelings. This will result in shadow versions and will appear clumsy, insincere, or even destructive.

To further illustrate the point about your psyche being out of balance, I will use a sports analogy. A few years ago, I watched as the Golden State Warriors etched their team into the history books by winning their second world championship in three years. Their opponent, and rival at the time, was the Cleveland Cavaliers, led by LeBron James, arguably the best basketball player in the world.

It seemed to be a common thought that, although Golden State had the most balanced team in the world, Cleveland had the "X factor," the best overall player in the league, LeBron James, which evened the score. Just as expected, LeBron James carried most of the workload.

Admittedly, he was magnificent in the series. However, his team was no match for the Golden State Warriors, who easily won the series in just four games.

With few exceptions, Golden State had the most balanced team I have ever seen. They had two, sometimes three solid players at each position. Each player was required to do only their part, play their role, and allow other team members to each play their own role. This balance allowed the team to move fluently, play comfortably, and rest when necessary.

On the other side, LeBron James was playing two, three, or even four different positions. In spite of being a top-notch, conditioned athlete, he would eventually tire from taking on too much. At times, he looked clumsy or out of place playing out of his natural position. His team was asking him to not only play his role, but everyone else's as well. The team was not balanced and relied heavily on LeBron James to restore it somehow. It did not work.

Just like any solid team, your psyche needs balance. Without balance, some parts of it will be forced to carry the load for the entire "team." The results are damaging. Because of your addiction, your psyche is working to restore the balance of anger, healthy selfishness, and troublemaking. Without making a conscious effort to honor our true-self, our psyche will use destructive methods to relieve the inner tension. Next, I will give you a couple of examples of how a shadow version of yourself develops. These examples are not the only possible outcomes, but you will probably recognize some of them.

Examples of Shadow Expression

Impulsive Anger

As I mentioned earlier, when a powerful emotion like anger is suppressed into the shadow, it does not disappear. It will eventually make itself known and often comes out as impulsive anger outbursts. I have worked with many clients who have trouble with impulsive anger. Often, what brings them to therapy is they cannot understand what makes them fly into a fit of rage over something seemingly insignificant. Many of these clients often have a very long fuse when it comes to anger, showing no overt signs of anger until it explodes. It's like a pressure cooker, building up until the psyche can no longer contain the energy. Then, seemingly out of the blue, a minor trigger such as a spouse coming home from work to find dirty dishes in the sink can blow the top off. In most cases, when the anger or destructive behavior subsides, these people are genuinely apologetic. What's more, they often adamantly deny being an "angry person."

Depression

Because anger is a very powerful form of energy, it can be a destructive energy, not only outwardly but internally as well. This internal destruction often presents as depression. Often, when people have all of this energy inside them but are unwilling to acknowledge it as anger, it will turn its destructive energy inward. It is true that depression can come from many places such as Vitamin D deficiency, thyroid dysfunction, and chemical imbalances. However, often it is anger that has not been expressed. Many of my clients who fall into a depression see themselves only as sad and depressed, not angry. However, I have seen depression vanish within weeks, sometimes days, if the depressed person is willing to own and discharge anger.

Irresponsible Spending

I once worked with a couple whom I will call Tom and Sally. Tom made the appointment and stated he needed marital counseling. Although I do not typically work with married couples, I agreed to meet with them. During the initial session, Sally reported she was very angry about how Tom had been spending their money.

Tom had a very expensive hobby, collecting vintage rare guitars. Sally mentioned that Tom had recently bought two vintage, and very expensive, guitars for his collection. Although they were in good financial shape, Sally feared she and Tom were not saving enough. She called Tom "very selfish."

However, Tom almost fell out of his chair in laughter when he asked her, "Are you kidding me? I pay for the house, the cars, the boat...everything you want, no matter what!" Although Tom felt that all he did was give her things, Sally saw his actions as indicative of not thinking more about the future. Tom was adamant he was selfless. Sally was convinced Tom was selfish. Helping Tom understand that his need to be selfish can be honored in ways that does not result in marital conflict was critical. This allowed him to have open conversations with his wife about carving out time for himself. As they worked together to ensure he had time for himself, he found impulsively spending money less desirable. Tom was owning his need for healthy selfishness rather than disowning and dumping this need into his shadow self.

Enabling

Enabling is basically doing things for others that they can, and should, do for themselves. Enabling is also a primary component in codependency. A codependent relationship is one in which there is excessive emotional or psychological reliance on another person. The dynamics of enabling mirror addiction almost perfectly. Believe it or not, enablers are very selfish in their actions. Consider a parent in a codependent relationship with a drug-addicted child. The addict has difficulty stopping the chemical due to fear of sobriety. She does not want to experience physical or social side effects or cope with real life without her drug of choice.

Likewise, enabling behavior happens because the enabler is essentially scared of the same things. They are unwilling or unable to cope with their lack of control over the situation. So they cope by getting a payoff or relief from anxiety each time they give into the demands of the addict.

Enablers will often justify these methods by convincing themselves they are just trying to help. The truth is, the only thing it helps is the enabler to feel better in the moment. It is, in fact, selfish, although most enablers would never identify it as such.

In these examples, people are clearly demonstrating the quality that they adamantly deny is a part of them. However, it is because they disown or do not acknowledge these qualities that they become defensive or they behave in a destructive way. When our suppressed and repressed qualities are presented in this way, they often are labeled very negatively by us and those around us: "He is such an angry jerk," "I'm just so selfish," "She causes so much trouble." These judgments only reinforce the notion that certain characteristics are wrong and should not be shown.

There are, of course, exceptions to this. Clearly, using anger to protect your loved ones would likely be seen as necessary or heroic rather than a character defect. I will discuss both the healthy and unhealthy ways to express our true-self throughout this book.

You have already learned about the "shadow" version of the self. However, in the next chapter, you will see just how destructive it can be.

Summary

In this chapter, you have learned about the characteristics of being a caretaker. You may even be beginning to see yourself as a caretaker. As I mentioned, we are all caretakers to some degree. However, constant accommodation will create a division in your psyche that will bury many qualities of your true-self. As I have mentioned, these buried feelings will eventually create chaos.

3

The Ego and Its Shadow

*Until you make the unconscious conscious, it will
direct your life and you will call it fate.*
—Carl Jung, psychiatrist

Carl Jung was a famous Swiss psychiatrist and psychoanalyst. Not only do I admire the above quote from Jung, I see the truth of it almost daily. Many of my clients often make remarks such as, "I guess I was just meant to be this way" or "I always knew I was going to be a screwup." They are talking as if there is some innate, predisposed condition that directs their lives. Maybe you have experienced a problem, but rather than explore it, you ignore it or complain about your luck.

I have found that when I am willing to explore the depths of my true-self, I gain insight beyond what I can imagine. However, developing this insight includes understanding that there is an internal division of the true-self. We will look closer at this division that consists of our ego and its shadow. In order to completely understand the shadow, however, you must first understand your psyche's ego.

Understanding the Ego

In this chapter, I will teach you the basic ideas behind the psyche's ego and the development of the shadow.

The ego is your sense of "me"—all your thoughts, feelings, and behaviors.

This will help you develop a clear understanding of how this division in the psyche hides many characteristics of your true-self. You will also learn which of these hidden qualities are vital to sustained recovery. First, let's further explore the concept of the ego.

I first heard the term "ego" as a young boy. If someone was acting arrogant or "cocky" someone might say, "she's got an ego!" In college, many years later, I would learn about the ego as defined by Sigmund Freud and other famous psychologists. It wasn't until I started working as a psychotherapist that I began to study the works of Carl G. Jung and, with it, his understanding of the ego. Admittedly, it is a difficult study because Carl G. Jung's writings are profound and often complicated. One could spend an entire career studying and interpreting his theoretical viewpoint.

However, I have come to understand that the Jungian concept of ego is simply what you are consciously aware of about yourself. The ego is how you define and/or describe who you are. It's everything you acknowledge is a part of yourself. All the feelings, thoughts, behaviors, interests, and beliefs that you allow yourself to own make up your ego. It is this definition of the ego that guides the way I formulate treatment.

As children we are taught, both directly and indirectly, and learn, both consciously and unconsciously, what is acceptable. These rules vary depending on the family. To survive, we adapt and own "acceptable" qualities that help construct our ego. For example, if being nice was highly valued in your family, you may believe you need to be a nice person. If you view yourself as a nice person, you have accepted and owned "nice" as part of your ego. Conversely, we are forced to deny or suppress "unacceptable" qualities even though they may be part of the true-self. Rather, these parts of the true-self get pushed deep into the unconscious and out of the ego's awareness.

Understanding the Shadow

As mentioned earlier, this dumping reservoir is called the "shadow." It takes energy for our ego to deny parts of our true-self and hold them in the shadow. Our ego will eventually become tired or distracted and will not be able to contain the shadow. So what happens then?

When the ego is no longer able to sustain the task of keeping the true-self hidden, the power of the shadow will eventually take over. It is when the emotion comes in its shadow form that we learn to fear it.

Robert's Story

I once worked with a man whom I will call Robert. He was spending nearly $400 a month replacing his cell phone. Here's the story about why he kept needing a new phone. When it came to anger, Robert had a very long fuse. He accommodated everyone and lacked any kind of assertive communication. But by making time for everyone else a priority, Robert left nothing for himself. He began to become resentful. Robert didn't see himself as an angry person, so when that feeling of resentment started to arise, he would avoid it. Robert's resentment grew into intense anger. However, this anger was left unacknowledged and thus kept in his shadow.

What Robert didn't know, but would later find out, was that he was a ticking time bomb. When Robert was caught off guard or very tired, his anger would erupt. Because he didn't like to hurt anyone, Robert would violently throw his phone, often shattering it. When he calmed down and the anger subsided, Robert felt ashamed for feeling angry. To top it off, he now had no cell phone and an expensive trip to the store.

Suggesting that there is healthy anger seemed ridiculous to Robert. He not only feared this emotion, he was ashamed and was unaware of how to appropriately express it. People like Robert only know what happens when the emotion pops up from an unknown place. Let me give you an analogy to further illustrate this.

When my son Grayson was very young, he had many toys to play with while taking his bath. One of his favorites was a group of five multicolored rubber floating ducks. I would often tease Grayson by submerging the ducks underwater so he could not see them. As he looked for the ducks, it became harder for me to keep all five of them submerged with one hand. Eventually, when one got away from my grasp, it shot out of the water, surprising both of us.

Think about this. Did those toy ducks disappear? Of course not, they were below the surface under water. They submitted to my restraining hand only temporarily. And when a duck did get away, it didn't slowly rise to the surface, it popped out of the water randomly and powerfully. Similarly, our true-self is not meant to be held down. Consider an example with a human emotion. I will use anger as the example because we have all seen its shadow forms in some way.

I spent many years working with children in a variety of settings. Having two children of my own, I am familiar with the temper tantrum. If you have not witnessed a child having a temper tantrum, I will give you a snapshot. The child begins by wanting something and being told no. If the child does not get what he or she wants, his or her rage leads to yelling, stomping, hitting, kicking, and throwing. Anyone who witnesses this would likely agree that anger can be a destructive, powerful, and sometimes physical emotional response.

When the ego is no longer able to sustain the task of keeping the true-self hidden, the power of the shadow will eventually take over. It is when the emotion comes in its shadow form that we learn to fear it.

The typical response from the parent or caretaker is punishment. If the intervention and/or punishment is appropriate, the child will learn that anger is okay and that there are healthy ways to express it. However, if the intervention and/or punishment is inappropriate, abusive, or neglectful, all the child will learn is that anger is bad.

For many, being "bad" is met with consequences. In such cases, children will attach fear and shame to the emotion, which causes problems later in life. In these cases, children feel they have no choice but to disown anger as part of their true-self. However, much like the submerged ducks, their anger will not disappear, it's just hidden from conscious awareness. The more energy these children use to hide their emotion, the more powerful it becomes while in the shadow.

So what do you suppose will happen when the suppressed emotion finally comes out? It will come popping out of the psyche with no predictable course or intensity. Moreover, the emotion may erupt in an overwhelming and powerful way—just like my son's toy duck. That duck didn't slowly rise to the surface after being forcefully submerged, it jumped out. Neither I nor my son could have predicted how the duck would behave as it jumped out of the water.

People typically see these shadow versions of emotion as being negative. What's worse, the emotions in these exaggerated forms will perpetuate the idea that they are bad, resulting in the psyche working harder to submerge them. The most common shadow manifestations of suppressed anger I come across are impulsive anger, depression and anxiety, panic attacks, and, yes, addiction. I will explain the causal relationship between suppressed anger and addiction later.

As I stated earlier, I believe all of us are victims of an upbringing in which parts of our true-selves are put down, not validated, or simply ignored altogether. We don't live in a perfect world. Even the best of parents and caretakers are just human. Being a parent myself helps me understand just how difficult it is to tend to every feeling or need my children have.

But we also live in a society that encourages denial of our true-self. Almost all of us have witnessed an athlete getting injured and covering his or her face to hide the vulnerability of pain. Or perhaps you have watched a sappy movie and during the emotional parts you fight back any visual display of sadness. We do these things because of our embarrassment or shame about what our showing emotion might say to others.

Those athletes or moviegoers are the same people who were very much spontaneous with emotions as young children. However, we learn early what feelings, emotions, behaviors, and dreams are "acceptable" and which are deemed "unacceptable." Later, as adolescents or adults, we witness shadow manifestations of emotions that further reinforce our belief that certain emotions are unacceptable.

Suppressing the True-Self

As I have mentioned, I believe there are three components of the true-self that, when suppressed, actually fuel addictive disorders. Specifically, these are anger, healthy selfishness, and troublemaking. I will spend significant time on all three components later. Each has tremendous value when utilized as intended. However, when suppressed, the shadow manifestations are not pleasant.

Anger, healthy selfishness, and troublemaking are enormously powerful and cannot be removed from the true-self. When these three powerful components of the true-self are submerged together, the psyche will eventually be overburdened, leading to potentially explosive behavior. The ego is not strong enough to keep all three components buried in the unconscious. When these three come together to erupt, what lies in the wake is an ocean of destruction. The destruction is often addiction.

When you have worked with addiction as long as I have, you learn one thing is certain: addiction is destructive. It's bound to cause trouble. I am referring to catastrophic consequences such as lost homes, lost careers, broken marriages, broken relationships with children, and even death. The irony for the addict is that they continue to be labeled as selfish, destructive, and a troublemaker, even as they strive to avoid making trouble that most of us would consider selfish and destructive. I understand these labels. I have personally interviewed the loved ones of the addicted clients with whom I work. I hear, in detail, the hell they're going through—hell caused by an addicted family member.

How Others See the Addicted Person

Interestingly, there is one observation I have made through all the years of working with addicted clients. Family members and loved ones invariably describe their addicted loved one as caring, soft, kind, and generous when sober. I cannot tell you how many times I have heard this exact statement: "What makes this so hard is that when he's not drinking, he is the most caring person you would ever meet. He would do anything for anyone."

What is actually happening is that while accommodating others, the addict has buried important parts of his or her true-self (anger, healthy selfishness, and troublemaking). However, when the ego gets drunk or high, the ability to submerge the true-self is nearly impossible. This often results in spontaneous eruptions of shadow versions of suppressed feelings, urges, and desires.

With an accommodating relationship style, a person is often seen as caring, selfless, and people-pleasing. They always put others first and agree with the masses, often withholding their own feelings and opinions. Therefore, those around them get their own needs met and remain happy. After all, wouldn't you like to be around someone who puts you first, allows you to have what you want, and never says no to you? This relational style works to the advantage of only one side. The accommodator's ego is tirelessly working to please others while neglecting his or her true-self. In fact, often when I begin working with folks in sobriety, they honestly have no idea what they like or what they want. Moreover, they have most certainly adopted the notion that anger, any selfishness, and troublemaking are "bad." That is, until I teach them how these very parts of the true-self are going to be their biggest allies in sobriety.

Summary

Your ego is everything you own and accept as a part of you. This includes: feelings, thoughts, behaviors, interests, and beliefs. They will sometimes be suppressed into the psyche's powerful shadow. With an understanding of your ego and its shadow, you have learned what happens if you ignore parts of your true-self and bury them. They do not disappear. They will only grow and eventually come out in a destructive way. It is time for you to dig into your shadow and learn how to make anger, healthy selfishness, and troublemaking your tools to sustained recovery.

Part II

Unlikely Friends:
Anger, Selfishness,
and Troublemaking

4

Redefining Anger

Anybody can become angry—that is easy, but to be angry with the right person and to the right degree and at the right time and for the right purpose, and in the right way—that is not within everybody's power and it is not easy.

—Aristotle, philosopher

With the exception of love, anger is the most powerful form of energy we have access to as human beings. Take a moment and consider what you think about anger. Do you think about only negative things? Perhaps road rage, violent behavior, or unpleasant interactions you have had with others. If these kinds of things are what come to mind, I would like to challenge the way you "filter" such concepts in your brain.

This chapter is the first of the three chapters devoted to exploring the key elements to help conquer your addiction. As previously mentioned, these "keys" are anger, healthy selfishness, and troublemaking. In this chapter, I will focus on anger. I will challenge you to "redefine" anger and use it constructively to help you stay sober. I will also give you practical methods you can use to access and express your anger.

Anger: A Powerful Emotion

Think about why we even have the ability to become angry. We were born with the amazing ability to be filled with this powerful emotion and utilize it. Anger is linked to great passion. When we are passionate about something, we are likely to fight for it. A client of mine recently visited Auckland, New Zealand. While there, she came across a sign that reminded her of the work we were doing together. Excited to share it with me, she took a picture of the caption, which read: "Love implies anger. The soul who is angered by nothing cares about nothing."

Anger is not the enemy. It is a tool, a weapon, and a friend, there for us to keep ourselves safe and healthy. Without being able to utilize this tool, we have no limits, no boundaries, nothing standing up for our own well-being.

This quote reminds me of when I used to work with couples in therapy. Many of them would come to therapy convinced the anger in their relationship would eventually destroy it. I would help these couples understand that it is apathy, not anger, that destroys relationships. As long as individuals care deeply, they will fight with great passion. However, if they become apathetic, any desire to engage is lost.

Early in my career I ran group therapy for men who were chemically addicted. Many of these men had very limited experience communicating on any intimate level. I would often ask men to report how they were feeling using a color rather than a word. Those who were feeling love or joy would often use the color red. Likewise, those who were feeling angry also used the color red. It must be that somewhere in us we instinctively understand a great connection between anger and passion.

Anger Helps Us Set Boundaries

Anger can also be a great defender of boundaries. Its purpose is to allow us to hold and push through limits. Anger is the energy that fights through pain. It "encourages" us to study rather than party, to exercise rather than watch television, and to challenge ourselves beyond our limits. Our ability to state an opinion, have a voice, stand up for and protect ourselves and others is dependent on having access to this energy. Anger gives us the ability to say no to unhealthy relationships, unnecessary spending, and destructive foods or chemicals. Without access to this energy and the ability to harness it for healthy use, we will feel powerless, tired, and fragile; we get walked on, and we voice no opinion. Anger is not an enemy. It is a tool, a weapon, and a friend, there for us to keep ourselves safe and healthy. Without being able to utilize this tool, we have no limits, no boundaries, nothing standing up for our own well-being.

Beth's Story

I once worked with a woman whom I will call Beth. She came to therapy to help her with her drinking problem. She was well educated and held a prestigious job at a local university. As a single mother, Beth worked hard to care for her two children, one of whom was disabled. Additionally, Beth was in a committed relationship with a man whom she wanted to marry. The problem for Beth was that these things she valued so much were being impacted by her drinking behavior.

Beth was, for all intents and purposes, a functional alcoholic. She was able to do her job and get her work done efficiently. Moreover, she was heavily involved in her children's lives and activities. With whatever energy she had left, Beth exhausted herself by trying to be the perfect girlfriend. To Beth, this role included taking care of her boyfriend and his three children financially and emotionally. At the end of each day, Beth had nothing left

Anger, when used constructively, is a healthy emotion that can help you protect yourself emotionally.

for herself. It was in the early evenings when she started to drink, and she wouldn't stop until she passed out.

I would regularly talk with Beth about how caring only for others, while seemingly noble, was neglecting her true-self and was therefore harmful to her. Beth was not using any of the energy necessary to hold boundaries with other people. This left no room for her to care for herself. Therefore, she had no awareness of her own feelings, wants, or needs. Because Beth had focused so much on others, the feelings she had of neglect and resentment were buried. Although she didn't realize it at the time, Beth turned to alcohol for "me time."

In therapy, Beth would eventually learn that lack of personal boundaries was highly destructive to her. We worked together to help her identify and express her own feelings, wants, and desires. For the first time, Beth began to feel the power of her frustrations and anger. She learned, with her newfound desire to take care of herself, she had to say no to the demands of others. She practiced assertiveness and limit setting. This became especially difficult with her boyfriend, who was accustomed to getting his every need met. When she would say no to one of his demands, he would ridicule her. She began to see how people, especially her boyfriend, were taking advantage of her generosity. This fueled her anger.

Now however, rather than bury her anger, she used it to put up a firm boundary with her boyfriend. Beth broke off the relationship and asked her boyfriend to move out. Weeks later, Beth used these skills to cut her abusive father out of her life. Beth was working diligently on her recovery, and she felt good about putting up boundaries. She almost didn't notice that her desire to drink at night had all but disappeared.

Consider an army whose job is to protect a king. A well-trained, disciplined, and honorable army will know what power they have and where and when to use it. The soldiers will understand that the purpose of their strength is to protect the king. Each soldier will be the aggressor only if necessary to fight for the king and kingdom. In doing so, the king is able to feel safe and secure. The kingdom will have boundaries protected by the army and soldiers willing to die to fight off enemy threats. Each decision the king makes will take into account that he has a strong and disciplined army.

However, if the army is strong and brave but lacks training, discipline, and honor, the king and kingdom are not secure. The soldiers will not be governed by the king. Their strength will be used to satisfy their own personal agendas and egos. This opens the door for destruction of the king and kingdom they are supposed to protect. The soldiers' feeble training will leave them with aggression but no direction, strength but no wisdom, and power but no honor. The result is a king and kingdom full of insecurities and fear of the army's power.

Ways to Acknowledge Your Anger

Too often we fear or simply do not properly acknowledge anger. Without understanding its true purpose, we run the risk of self-destruction. If we do not use anger to help establish personal boundaries, we will feel anxious and insecure.

For those suffering with addiction, access to healthy anger is severely compromised. There is no security either within themselves or in their physical space. Their limits are easily penetrated by chemicals and there are no boundaries in their personal relationships. Rather than suppressing this energy, they need to experience and express it while sober. In doing so, they will learn how to harness it in order to set limits, maintain boundaries, and feel safe and secure. They need to develop the "army" inside of them and train it to be utilized to protect their inner "king."

In the text that follows, I will give you examples of specific actions you can do to get in touch with anger. In doing so, you can learn how to use it to your advantage, set limits, hold boundaries, and go after what you want. Also, you can protect your true-self and feel more powerful and secure. These examples are not in order of importance or degree of difficulty. All the examples are beneficial. Begin where you are most comfortable.

Journal Writing

The potential benefits to journal writing are vast. Regular journaling can help you prioritize goals, stay on track, increase problem solving, and cope with stress. Perhaps most importantly, journaling can help you fully know and care for your true-self. Of course, caring for your true-self includes acknowledging all of your emotions.

To use the energy of anger, you will need to know how you experience it within yourself. Writing about irritations, frustrations, or things that make you angry can help you do this. Try to write down instances, people, or other things that make you angry. The triggers can range from a minor annoyance to a life situation that enrages you. Begin to pay attention to all things that bring up angry energy, whether they are big or small. Try to get in touch with each physical sensation and learn more about how they present within you. In doing so, you will also be able to more easily recognize specific triggers to your anger.

Occasionally, some people are not actually aware of what annoys, irritates, or enrages them. Perhaps you are one of these people. In this case, focus on body sensations, particularly in the chest, neck, shoulders, arms, and hands. If you feel tension, tightness, or pressure, focus on the frequency and intensity of the sensation. Once focused, write them down. This will help you stay with the emotion rather than move away from it.

When writing about the sensations you experience, it also helps to give each sensation specific adjectives. Try to give the sensations you feel a color, shape, or size. Recognizing these body patterns can give you clues to what triggers anger. When you are clued in, you can learn to recognize anger and express it appropriately. Let me teach you some of the ways you can do this.

Saying No

When my children first learned to say no, it felt so good to them, that they were saying no to things they actually wanted. Why? For the first time, they felt power. It felt so good for them to set a limit, they kept using it even when they didn't even know what they were saying no to.

For many of us, the idea of holding a limit and saying no is very anxiety-provoking. It can even feel as though we are hurting someone's feelings. Some people can even feel inner conflict if they say no to anyone or anything. This can be especially true with loved ones.

However, just as my children learned, there is strength and power behind saying no and setting limits. In doing so, we are holding boundaries and taking care of ourselves. This will eventually lead to feeling more secure within our physical space, as well as internally. Practicing saying no can and will transfer to feeling confident and secure in setting limits related to chemical use. This includes confronting or avoiding people and places that trigger use of drugs or alcohol.

However, there are instances in which saying no feels too overwhelming for people. Perhaps you feel this way and simply the thought of saying no is anxiety-inducing. In this case, I suggest you start by noticing every time you actually wanted to say no but rather said yes. The urge to say no is a signal for you to put up and hold a limit. Try to be consciously aware of when there is an urge to set a boundary.

I once worked with a twenty-one-year-old college student whom I will call Jessica. She could not even entertain the idea of saying no to her friends who consistently asked her to party with them. She had developed a severe binge drinking problem and knew accommodating her friends was perpetuating it. Knowing this, however, did not stop the severe anxiety she experienced when thinking about her friends' reactions if she rejected their invitation. In fact, she kept drinking with her friends in spite of a strong desire to stop.

Over time, Jessica accepted the importance of setting limits. She started small. She began making a list of everything she did to accommodate her friends and began saying no in the situations that brought the least anxiety. Eventually she was able to work up the list and use this skill to stop herself from being coaxed to go to a party.

This simple skill not only helped Jessica stop abusing alcohol, but helped her set healthy limits with study time, work, and in relationships.

Physical Expression

Physical expression is simply using your body to express your emotion. For example, if you were to punch a wall in a fit of anger, you would be expressing your anger physically. Encouraging a physical expression of anger for therapeutic purposes is controversial. I have known well-trained psychologists who believe that being aggressive in any way will increase the possibility of more aggression. In other words, some believe that rather than using aggression to "discharge" your anger, you will actually become more aggressive indefinitely. Some will even argue that simply watching aggressive activities will have a similar effect. I tend to disagree.

I have very little fear that learning how to express anger in a physical, yet controlled, manner will lead to more anger and aggression. By controlled I mean you are in charge of where, when, and how you express your anger. I have seen no evidence in my clinical practice that expressing anger in a healthy way produces longer, more intense, feelings of anger. On the contrary, when my clients work hard to be physically aggressive in a controlled and safe environment, relief is typically the outcome.

Relief, along with fatigue, is also what follows the temper tantrum of a child. I have seen this many times observing my own children. Either child could have a full-blown tantrum, with flailing hands, stomping feet, and screaming and yelling. Once calm though, they are running around and playing. Sometimes, they even forget the reason they were mad. To me, this is proof that after an emotion runs through us, it ceases to have any power over our thinking or behavior. Our bodies are designed to take the intensity of the emotion and express it through various behaviors.

Many people, however, have never learned how to fully access the physical form of anger. This means that many of us were never allowed to have a temper tantrum or yell and scream while feeling angry. The reason for this is because anger and temper tantrums were dangerous for many of us as children. I say dangerous because this emotion, and subsequent behaviors, were often met with punishment rather than used to educate appropriate anger expression. Punishments such as grounding, shunning, yelling, or shaming can result in a child fearing their own anger and stopping the pathways of anger from fully developing.

As an adult, however, you have the power to take control of your behavior. You can express anger and experience what it feels like to have this power without judgment or shame. There are many exercises that will effectively give you this capability. I tend to teach three of them as I believe they are the most effective.

Exercising for Expressing Controlled Anger

The first exercise is an adult temper tantrum exercise in which an adult lies on a bed or mattress and essentially throws a tantrum. This allows the person to be consciously aware, moderately in control, and safely feel this energy that has been locked up.

The second exercise involves kneeling down in front of a bed or couch. Hold both hands together like you are praying; then, hold your arms above your head. Now strike the mattress or pillow with your folded hands. Repeat several times.

Lastly, I have often asked people to buy a heavy bag and hit and kick it ten to fifteen minutes per day. These heavy bags are the same ones used by martial artists, boxers, and physical trainers and are available at almost any sporting goods store.

All three of these exercises move the energy in a constructive direction, rather than direct the energy inward. You can also be creative with this process. I had a client once who reported the only thing that satisfied her anger was the sound of breaking glass. She had spent several hundred dollars on new cell phones and televisions as a result of her outbursts of anger. We discussed the need for her to be safe and healthy yet satisfy her boiling anger. She came up with the idea to visit every garage sale she could find and buy up old cheap glass objects. She set up a space in her garage, put on safety glasses, and destroyed every piece of glass.

The contructive expression of anger is not only healthy, but essential for your recovery.

As you might remember from science class, energy cannot just disappear. It can only be moved. If we do not learn to move anger outward in the direction where it is intended, it will move inward causing chaos and destruction. Examples of this chaos and destruction include: anxiety, panic disorder, depression, impulsive anger, and addiction.

Of course, the goal is for you to know and understand anger, not be afraid of it. I want you to understand and express anger in a healthy way. Then you will be able to draw on it when necessary to set up limits and boundaries. These limits and boundaries are essential in recovery. You must use limits to put space between yourself and destructive places, people, and chemicals.

When you begin to challenge yourself in this way, you can get to a place where the feeling is so good you never want to go back to suppressing anger. More importantly, when this energy is incorporated into the ego's awareness, there is no pressure developing in the shadow. Therefore, the potential for a destructive version of the emotion is drastically decreased. What is left is a healthy way of using anger as it was designed. This is very good news for anyone whose self-destruction has taken the form of addiction.

Summary

I hope by now you can see why the constructive expression of anger is not only healthy, but essential for your recovery. Recovering from addiction requires that you do not allow yourself to be controlled by anything destructive. This can happen only if you have healthy access to your anger and use it to put up limits and boundaries.

Think of yourself as being your own "king" or "queen." As you practice these anger expression exercises, remind yourself that this energy is there to protect the "kingdom" of you!

5

Redefining Selfishness

Be who you are and say how you feel, because those who mind don't matter, and those who matter don't mind.

—Dr. Seuss

I remember when the Oxford dictionary chose "selfie" as the word of the year. I can't say I was surprised—it seems we live in a culture that is becoming more and more obsessed with "me." Consistent messages from peers and social media seem to give us more reasons to focus on ourselves. In spite of this, however, many of us would rather not be labeled as selfish. I find it interesting that even though we are seemingly infatuated with ourselves, many of us often view selfishness as a deplorable quality. We may even loosely attach the label of narcissism to those we consider to be selfish.

Healthy Selfishness

So, as you can imagine, introducing the concept of needing to be selfish can be met with much resistance. Although I understand why many people may be resistant to the idea of needing to be more selfish, I believe the resistance is based on how one defines selfishness. This is why I educate my clients about the difference between healthy selfishness and unhealthy selfishness.

This chapter will focus entirely on healthy selfishness, which is really just good self-care. You will learn how living an accommodating life will lead to profound self-harm and continued addictive behavior. I am going to teach you why self-care is a necessary component to sobriety. This chapter will also introduce several practical methods you can use to increase your self-care.

Self-Care

Self-care is not the same thing as being self-absorbed, arrogant, or narcissistic. It is possible to focus on yourself and take into account the well-being of others as well. However, before I discuss how to do this and why it is so important, I want you to understand how most of us develop our point of view of the "self." It involves a keen understanding of the difference between the true-self and what I refer to as the "what-self."

The "What-Self"

As you may recall, the true-self includes desires, feelings, needs, urges, and dreams. It's who you are and all the unique qualities about you. In America, however, we do not do a very good job of honoring who we are or who others are. We suppress our urges and feelings, shun our dreams, and are out of touch with our desires. We talk in terms of material wants and seek guidance from television, magazines, social media, and peers. This socializing of how we should feel or what we ought to want cripples the true-self. It is because of this that many of my clients have no genuine desire for anything other than what they are taught they should want. I submit to you that the reason for this is that there is limited or no value put on honoring the true-self.

Sadly, the result is we learn to take on a persona. A persona is a way of presenting to the world who we are. It is often not our true-self, but rather a collection of what we think we should present to people. Our personas often consist of learned wants, skills, ideas, and behaviors. This identity based on what others teach us we should be is what I refer to as the "what-self." It may also be considered a "false-self." When people define themselves in this way, their esteem often rises and falls based on outside influences such as job performance, pleasing people, material objects, and relationships. Moreover, these individuals tend to develop a very narrow definition of who they are.

Self-care is not the same as being self-aborded, arrogant, or narcissistic. It is possible to focus on yourself and take into account the well-being of others as well.

For example, I used to run a daily therapy group for men who were in a residential treatment facility. As each group began, I asked each member to tell a little about who they are. Many of these men had years of exposure to the Alcoholics Anonymous (AA) community. Those in AA groups tend to introduce themselves in this way, "Hello, I'm Jeff and I'm an alcoholic." I knew this description is nowhere near a quality of the true-self, therefore I did not allow them to introduce themselves in this way. Rather, I had them introduce themselves in this way, "Hello, my name is Jeff."

Those men in my therapy group could not identify and own one genuine quality of their true, authentic self to introduce to the group. Upon further inquiry, I discovered they enjoyed golfing, fishing, or playing piano; however, these are all learned skills. Although the desire to acquire these skills is a component of the true-self, the actual skills of athletics, hobbies, or music are not.

Many of my clients have been acknowledged for only learned skills and behaviors. If the behavior or skill is acknowledged as good, the person feels they are good. However, if the behavior or skill is acknowledged as bad, the person feels they are bad. In these cases, a person is unable to separate the "who" and the "what" self. He or she views what they do as precisely who they are, just as the men in my therapy group did.

For example, suppose when my children had temper tantrums I used only punishment as a way of calling out their behavior. Now imagine they received the same response across other areas of their life such as at their grandparents' house, at school, or in the community. Both of my children would most likely associate anger with trouble. This would reinforce a fear of their own anger or a desire to keep anger hidden. However, if the emotional response to the tantrums is separated from the poor behavior, there would be no need to fear the actual emotion.

For example, I can talk to my children about how a tantrum is an unacceptable behavior and use appropriate punishments to try and stop such behavior. At the same time, however, I can acknowledge that their anger is healthy, even appropriate, and encourage appropriate ways of expressing it. I am not excusing poor choices or dismissing destructive behavior. I am teaching them that behavior does not define them. By doing this, I communicate to them that there is a distinct difference between who they are and what they do.

Think about your own life. Think about how often loved ones support and acknowledge who you are or what you need, in spite of your poor behavior. Or even more importantly, how often do you separate who you are and what you do? Remember, a person is not born with the skills or knowledge to be a physician, a great athlete, or a successful businessperson. These are all learned skills that exist separate from the innate feelings, needs, desires, and dreams of their true, authentic self. Moreover, because skills alone are not fulfilling to the true-self, we continually strive to achieve more, collect more, buy more, and do more to try and fill the void. This paves the way to boast in the false-self and exhibit shadow versions of selfishness such as narcissism and addiction. So what then is healthy selfishness or good self-care?

One of the best analogies I can think of to help illustrate healthy selfishness, or self-care, is the use of oxygen masks on an airplane. As you may know, prior to takeoff the flight attendants give instructions to be followed in the event of an emergency. They demonstrate how to use the oxygen masks that drop from above your seat in the event that cabin pressure gets too low. After they instruct you on how to use the mask, they emphasize what you must do first: Put your own mask on! It is only when your mask is on correctly that you are in a position to help children and others. After all, how can you help other passengers if you can't breathe?

Being healthy requires you to take care of yourself first. This is not a mean or destructive quality, it's a healthy one. When you learn to properly care for yourself, you are better equipped to help others. More importantly, there is a conscious recognition and ownership of the need for self-care, thus decreasing the chances of a shadow manifestation to erupt, which often results in a unhealthy, and destructive version of selfishness.

The problem for those who suffer with addiction is that they do not have a strong history of developing and maintaining self-care. This is exacerbated by the fact that the addict is usually being consistently ridiculed for their perceived selfishness. In all fairness, addiction is, quite frankly, very selfish. As a client of mine once put it, "When I'm drunk I say what I want and do what I want. I don't have to worry about my bills, my relationships, or any responsibilities. It's like a vacation in a bottle." Not only is this a selfish escape from reality, but the person often doesn't even take ownership of their need for any kind of selfishness by justifying self-serving behavior with a statement such as, "I was just drunk." Statements like these perpetuate the inner belief that the individual exists separate from the feeling. Making a conscious effort to own an emotion is practicing self-care and is a critical part of reaching and sustaining sobriety.

Over the years, I have used many different methods to help clients with self-care. Some of these methods I will detail at the end of this chapter. It starts, however, with knowing who you are. By this I mean owning your feelings, knowing your desires, and paying attention to your urges. It is important to note that this does not mean you demand everything you desire and follow all of your urges. Part of being a mature adult involves understanding how to compromise with others as well as understanding we can't always have what we desire. It is important, however, to know what your true feelings, urges, and desires actually are. This helps in learning how to value these things and also use insight to follow what they may be telling you about yourself.

I often see clients who not only cannot tell me how they feel or what they want, but they don't even know themselves. This is heartbreaking. A person cannot possibly value a sober existence if they have no sense of how to value who they are when sober.

Knowing Yourself

How well do you know yourself? Take a brief self-assessment. How do you feel right now? How do you know? Where do you feel it? What does this feeling tell you? Do you know your deepest desires or strongest passions? Do you keep a journal of your feelings and dreams? All we have to do is pay attention to the things that naturally happen within us.

Think about how you get to know someone. You choose to spend time with them and understand what they are about. We must use the same method with ourselves. We need to spend quality time with ourself and "get to know me." The skills at the end of this chapter will provide examples on how to do this. However, spending good time with ourselves is foreign to most people who have never been valued or have to escape their own company through addiction.

Have you ever heard or said, "I'm bored"? We throw that term around without thinking about what it actually means. But when you say you are bored you are essentially saying, "I'm in my own company and I can't stand it." This is a total rejection of one's self.

Developing a healthy self involves being selfish and demanding quality time with your innermost desires, feelings, and urges. It's about consistently paying attention to ourselves. As you may already know, the more you pay attention to something, the harder it is to ignore.

A person cannot possibly value a sober existence if they have no sense of how to value who they are when sober.

For example, I have been involved in weight training since I was a teenager. Throughout the years I have strained muscles, broken fingers, torn ligaments, and developed arthritic joints. Most days, I have some kind of physical pain. On very busy work days, I may be so distracted that I hardly notice the various, lingering pains. However, when the distractions are gone at the end of the day, I sit down to relax and all of a sudden I notice my sore body. The more I pay attention to it, the more intense it gets. Although here I am referring to physical pain, this is true for most anything we focus on, including thoughts and emotions.

In sobriety, the longer people remove the chemical that allows them escape, the more of themselves they will have to deal with. If they do not know anything about themselves, it can feel like conversing with an odd or threatening stranger. Rarely do people push through the discomfort to fully know and value who they are. However, it is necessary for sobriety to eliminate distractions and focus on yourself. This may be new or anxiety-provoking for you, but if you can push through any reluctance, the rewards are plentiful. Following are some methods to begin to know and understand more of your wants, desires, needs, and feelings.

Window-Shopping

This may sound a bit unusual to many, but the truth is that many people have no idea what they like. Their accommodating relational style has them focused only on what others like, want, or need. I talk to people all the time who could create lists of what their parents or spouses want or need. However, when it comes to themselves, they have no clue. We all need to develop a sense of what we actually like, independent of what others think we should like or dislike. We need to be able to confidently hold an actual opinion.

For many of my clients who do not know themselves well, I will ask them to go window-shopping. I will instruct them to go to a shopping center by themselves and start selecting things they like. It's important to note I am not asking them to buy anything. In fact, I often specifically ask them to not buy anything. This is simply an exercise to develop an internal focus on their own opinions and likes. Often, the client returns to therapy the following week reporting how difficult this task actually was. Rather than focusing entirely on what they like or want, they had intrusive thoughts about what others would think about it. I often continue to encourage them to practice this method, while reassuring them it will get easier.

Remember, with this window-shopping exercise, there is no interaction with others at this point. This is an internal exercise. You don't necessarily have to go to a store. You can practice on the Internet or look through a magazine. The important point is to practice actually having an opinion that comes from within you. If you can, try to notice what you actually like about the items you pick. The more you can practice holding these opinions, the better equipped you will be to hold opinions on more-important issues.

Journaling

Journaling has already been mentioned as a tool for dealing with anger. You can use your "anger journal" or keep a separate one for "self-care." Either way, the important thing is that you are getting your feelings out on paper. Journaling is one of the best ways to totally turn your attention toward yourself. There are no rules and no grading for punctuation, grammar, or spelling. The process is not about how you write but about keeping a record of your feelings.

Through journaling you can write about feelings, entertain fantasies, and explore desires. Journaling can be organized or unorganized. You can write letters to yourself or to others, but you don't have to mail the letters. Your journal can take the form of words or images. Many people keep a sketch pad and draw or color what they feel within them. This is a time in which you can honor anything that is happening within you. This is a sacred space that nobody gets to penetrate. It allows you space to practice self-care and be completely open. If you have never written in a journal before, I suggest you get a few notebooks.

Start by sitting in a quiet space where you will be uninterrupted for at least ten to fifteen minutes. Begin by writing about whatever comes to mind. It may be a thought, feeling, or even an image. Suspend self-judgment or concern. There is absolutely no right or wrong. When you begin to get more comfortable journaling, you may have specific issues to write about. Anything you need or want to say is important and appropriate. It's all for you and is not meant to be shared with anyone.

Because many people are so far removed from understanding their own true-selves, journaling can be a difficult task. Some individuals have never had their feelings, thoughts, needs, or opinions validated. Doing so can create discomfort. It is very important for you to remember that everything you write is valuable because you are valuable. Here are some questions to ask yourself as you start to journal.

- How do I feel?
- What makes me angry, sad, joyful, or embarrassed?
- If I could snap my fingers and have a perfect life, what would it look like?
- What is my biggest fear?
- What am I passionate about?
- If I had to sell myself for a job interview, what would I include?
- What do I love about me?
- Why is it hard to be me?

As you can imagine, the possibilities are endless. Give yourself a fair shot. You will not regret it. Journaling about these things is self-care and will help you get to know yourself better. Caring for yourself is essential to recovery.

Identifying Feelings

As I have already stated, feelings are a large part of the true-self. Part of practicing self-care includes being in touch with your feelings. I have worked with some people who have no idea what their feelings are. This is not surprising considering the academic, workaholic, money-driven society we live in. Our children are being taught more about how to use their brains than their hearts.

I really like teaching feeling identification because the science behind it is so fascinating. With advances in modern medicine, we know that both the heart and the gut have many neuroreceptors. That is, when certain events happen in our lives, neurons fire from the brain and connect with these receptors like a lock and key in the heart and gut to create body sensations. We have been using terms like "heartache" and "gut feeling" instinctively for centuries. Now we actually know why. All feelings have a specific body pattern with physical sensations. In order to identify a feeling, one must pay attention to these sensations.

Try the following process to practice this internal focus. First, close your eyes. Turn your attention to the space between your neck and waist. Do you notice any feelings or sensations? If so, it's not necessary to name them, just to be aware of them. Now, concentrate on these sensations and use adjectives to describe their size, shape, or color to further explore the feeling. Are they tiny, huge, red? If you begin to move your attention into your head, just refocus on your body.

By exploring the feeling completely, you are in a better position to actually label it. This labeling may be easy for some; however, many people come from environments where their feelings were often disregarded or punished, or they have spent many years numbing their feelings with chemicals. For them, developing the skill to explore and label their feelings requires taking healthy risks, practice, and patience.

When I am helping a client as they begin a feeling identification exercise, I ask that they stay within the five feelings categories I give them and use only these. I believe it keeps people focused on the feeling rather than searching their minds for the perfect label for it. The five feeling categories are:

- Anger
- Sadness
- Embarrassment
- Love/Joy
- Fear

At first it may be difficult to know if your body is actually having an emotion or just experiencing a different physical reaction such as indigestion. Be patient and consistent. Over time, you will learn to distinguish the difference.

Meditation

Meditative practices have been used for centuries. In more recent years, scientific advances have allowed us to develop actual proof of meditation's efficacy for a variety of issues including both physical and emotional pain. In spite of both wisdom and science, most people I talk with have not incorporated a meditative practice into their life. They focus on people, chemicals, material goods, money, stressors, and many other things outside themselves. Meditation brings attention back inward toward the self. Having a regular meditative routine can reduce or even eliminate negative thoughts such as, "I'm worthless" or "I'm dumb." Meditation can also help resolve such issues as anxiety, depression, and even chronic pain.

In spite of meditation being a relatively simple technique, it can be quite difficult for some people. Many people have been distracted for many years by external factors such as family, school, jobs, peer relationships, and financial burdens. In addition, they can become overwhelmed by automatic intrusive thoughts that lead to increased stress, anxiety, or depressed moods.

Take a moment to explore where the majority of your time or attention goes. If you have difficulty doing this, write down what your weekly schedule is and where your time goes. You may find that you are habitually "busy," focusing on external factors or intrusive thoughts rather than on self-care. For example, you may find that you spend a lot of time worrying about things you cannot control. Or perhaps you use up time in front of the television that could be better spent focusing on self-care.

Changing some of these habits can be difficult, primarily because self-care requires focus and deliberate practice. By this, I mean you must deliberately make time to focus on your true-self. Meditation is a great way to do this and practice calming life's distractions. You have to be willing to practice on a daily basis and resist the urge to quit if you become distracted. Try the following exercise to get a sense of what a brief meditation can feel like.

Sit in a comfortable chair with your feet flat on the ground. Place the palm of one hand on your chest and the palm of your other hand across your belly button. Now take a deep breath, pushing the air all the way down to your belly, allowing it to fill up like a balloon. Your hand on your belly should move up slowly as air fills your abdomen. Your hand on your chest should not move at all. Pause very briefly, and exhale with no force, allowing the air to move out slowly. After you get a good feel for this, begin to inhale for a count of five, then exhale for a count of five. Continue this for several minutes.

When you breathe, focus on your breath coming in and moving out. Picture the air moving in and out. Your mind may get distracted at first. You may think of other things, notice sounds, or even have a distracting body sensation. This is okay. Just notice whatever is distracting you and redirect focus back on your breathing.

I suggest you try to be focused in this way for two to five minutes each day. As you continue to practice, see if you can stretch the time to ten or fifteen minutes each day. If you do, you will be well on your way to developing a good meditation practice. This simple technique is just the tip of the iceberg. If you become interested in advanced meditative practices, I suggest you explore the local library, bookstore, or search online. There are thousands of books written on various meditation techniques.

Dream Work

In all my years of training, nothing is more intriguing to me than dream work. Dreams are beautiful windows into our unconscious minds. As our body sleeps, our mind is still trying to work things out and often grabs our attention through dreams. However, many people do not pay any attention to their dreams. We often talk about them only if they are disturbing nightmares. For many people, these nightmares consist of them being in some kind of grave danger. The unconscious is so adamant that you pay attention that it may threaten you with death! Of course, we do not die and our unconscious minds are not attempting to kill us.

If we pay more attention, we may discover what the message actually is. In my experience with dream analysis, I find if people pay attention to their dreams they are astonished at what they discover. It opens up an entire new world and helps clients gain an understanding of what their conscious mind is suppressing or ignoring. To understand your dreams, you first need to remember them. I suggest keeping a dream journal right beside your bed. Immediately after you wake up, write down any details of any dream you had that night. If you do not write it down immediately, you will likely forget most or all the detail as the day progresses.

You will also need a way to help you analyze and interpret the dreams you log. I suggest finding a therapist who has experience with dream work. However, if you are interested in learning the basics of dream work and exploring on your own, I highly suggest reading *Inner Work: Using Dreams and Active Imagination for Personal Growth* by Robert A. Johnson.

Guided Imagery

Guided imagery has been used to help people with various issues from stress relief and relaxation to enhancing performance in academics, employment, or athletics. One of the biggest reasons that imagery has such a powerful effect is because it is, in fact, creating an experience.

For example, look around the room you are in. Any chair, desk, television, phone, frame, or artwork was once an idea inside someone's imagination before becoming the thing in your room. Someone had to use their imagination to design the chair you are sitting in before it ever became a real tangible thing. In other words, they already had the experience mentally of building a chair; it just had to get put together. Using your imagination to help enhance your life will eventually play out in real time.

As a psychotherapist, I see this regularly with clients who are constantly imagining negative things. These people spend all day with fears that they will be crippled in some way, which results in chronic anxiety and/or depression for them. These chronic mood issues end up crippling them emotionally.

The goal for you is to use imagery so you can have positive experiences daily. A great way to do this is through a technique called "positive rehearsal." Essentially, positive rehearsal is imagining yourself exactly where you want to be. For example, I have counseled many doctoral students over the years and many of these students are highly anxious about finishing their studies. Using positive rehearsal, I help them mentally create the desired outcome. I walk them through each moment of their day, everything from what they are going to wear to what they will eat for lunch. Each detail is imagined with power, confidence, and peace. I ask that they do this daily. By the time they have to finish an academic task, they will have had multiple experiences with succeeding at it.

Re-Parenting Exercise

The concept of re-parenting involves a person taking care of themselves in a way that is consistent with healthy parenting. There are a variety of exercises used by therapists all around the globe. The one I would like to share with you involves imagery. It is incredibly powerful and will help you develop your true-self. I call it the "re-parenting" exercise. It's easy to memorize and I take clients through it during sessions with them and then ask that they do it every day. When clients actually commit to this, I cannot overstate my amazement at how rapidly they begin to recognize and express their true-self.

Take a few minutes to try the re-parenting exercise. It can be life changing. All it takes is a comfortable setting, minimal noise, and five minutes. It goes like this:

Imagine that standing in front of you is a child. Picture the age, gender, eye color, hair color, clothing, and so on. Continue until you have the entire image pictured perfectly. Now picture an adult coming into the scene and giving the child a task to accomplish. The child is told that their worth and value as a human being is completely dependent on their ability to complete this task. What the child is not told is that this task is impossible. No child can do it; no adult can do it.

Now picture this child trying this task and failing, trying and failing, trying and failing. Picture the facial expression and emotion as this child is so desperately trying this task and failing. Now shift all your attention to you. Imagine you walk into this scene. You know exactly what is going on. You know exactly what that child is going through and what that child needs. Now picture yourself giving that child exactly what you know, in your heart, that child needs at that moment.

Open your eyes when you are ready. I am guessing you knew exactly what that child needed. When I am doing this exercise with clients, an overwhelming majority of the time they tearfully acknowledge the child's need for love and acceptance. This often happens as they imagine the adult in the image hugging this child. I would encourage you to continue this imagery daily, keeping in mind what your heart told you was appropriate for the child.

It is important to note that some people will imagine they are actually trying to complete the task for the child. In these cases, I often challenge the client to think about why this response can actually be damaging because focusing on completing the task only highlights the importance of the task. This imagery is about valuing the child independently of anything he or she can accomplish.

All of these activities can be used as tools to help you discover your true-self. By setting aside time to do them, you are practicing healthy self-care. Along with that comes benefits such as increased confidence and feeling better both emotionally as well as physically. Most importantly, as I have mentioned already, self-care is essential to maintain sobriety.

The more you focus on self-care, the stronger you will understand your own needs. In the process, you will be building a stronger relationship with yourself. Just like other personal relationships, not everything about this is always fun, positive, and comfortable. While focusing on self-care, you will discover both joy and comfort as well as pain and discomfort. One of the painful, yet necessary, issues you may encounter is grief.

Expressing Grief

Grief is uncomfortable. We often try to distract ourselves from the pain of grief. However, unresolved grief will weight you down and ultimately rob you of joy. One of my favorite Latin phrases is *si vis pacem, para bellum* which is translated as "if you want peace, prepare for war." Grief can often feel like a battle, but it is necessary to reach peace and closure. As you learn more about what your needs are, you may experience grief about how those needs were or are being neglected. This neglect can be a result of your early experiences and/or your current behavior. Additionally, you may experience grief related to giving up the chemical that has become your predictable and consistent coping method.

Often, I see addicts in recovery who try to convince themselves or others that they do not want a chemical they have become dependent on. Many of these people are lying to themselves or falling back into accommodating what others would like to hear. Sure, it is nice to hear, "That drug was such a horrible thing, I am never going to use again," but this is rarely the truth. Many addicts have spent years in behavior that suggests drugs are all they want to do. In order to properly treat addiction, you must acknowledge that you, or at least part of you, wants to use drugs. This is significant because coming to terms with wanting to have something and not being allowed to have it results in grief. Self-care includes owning the desire to use your drug of choice in order to process the loss of it.

Summary

As I have stressed throughout this chapter, self-care is essential for sustained recovery. It begins with challenging the notion that self-care is destructive or "selfish." Good self-care includes developing a strong relationship with your true-self to value "who" you are rather than define yourself by what you do. Remember: As you practice talking care of yourself, you will get to know yourself entirely—the "good, the bad, the ugly." As you continue to practice self-care, your feelings, needs, and desires will be harder to ignore. This yields confidence, which is necessary for good health and sobriety.

6

Redefining
Troublemaking

*And I not only have the right to stand up for myself,
but I have the responsibility.*
— Maya Angelou, civil rights activist

We currently live in a society in which we develop a love–hate relationship with troublemaking. It seems none of us wants trouble to disrupt our own life, but we are more than willing to be entertained by stories about conflict in the media.

We may be glad that trouble is not happening to us, but we are certainly intrigued by it. Why do we like to witness trouble but not experience trouble? Perhaps we simply like entertainment no matter where it comes from. Maybe life is mundane and drama gives us something to talk about. Or maybe it makes us somehow feel superior when others engage in conflict.

Although any of these reasons are entirely possible, I hold a different opinion. I believe many people do not integrate troublemaking characteristics into their ego. Therefore, the components of troublemaking, which are a part of them, are buried in their shadow. Why do we tend to bury these troublemaking characteristics in the shadow? It stems from how we learned to define troublemaking.

This chapter will help you understand how your accommodating relationship style is related to the need to make trouble. Therefore, we will revisit some of what was learned about accommodation. All accommodators want to avoid trouble. I will teach you why it feels so scary to cause trouble as well as methods you can use to regain a healthy troublemaking skill set.

For those in active addiction, there is constant chaos and trouble interwoven into their lives. If and when they become sober, they are constantly reminded by loved ones or the legal system of all the trouble they have caused. Often, there is evidence of their troublemaking such as wrecked cars, loss of jobs, loss of relationships, and criminal behavior.

Suggesting people need to become troublemakers in order to heal may seem ridiculous to someone who has been labeled a troublemaker for much of their life. That is, unless you are willing to expand how you define troublemaking.

Take a moment and notice what comes to mind when you think of a troublemaker. For many, the thoughts or images of troublemaking are negative. Maybe you think of a criminal, a jokester, or even a Hollywood child character like Kevin McCallister from the movie *Home Alone*. Or maybe, rather than negativity, you find yourself thinking of the "bad boy" appeal.

No matter what comes to your mind, you have certain images or beliefs about "troublemakers."

Beliefs Developed in Childhood

As I already mentioned, many of these beliefs about troublemakers begin early in childhood and are based on relational experiences. Whether you know it or not, you are terrified of causing trouble. However, the trouble I am talking about is actually referring to being assertive and honoring your true-self. Being assertive sounds easy, right? Think again. Let's take a closer look as to why this is actually quite difficult to accomplish.

As you may remember from chapter 2, the accommodating relational style develops out of necessity. An infant or toddler brain does not have the ability to make rational decisions or consider logical conclusions. The part of their brain responsible for rational thinking, the prefrontal cortex, is still developing and will continue to develop well into early adulthood. Therefore, the child must rely on instinct. Instinct is a "gut" feeling or programmed response.

For example, it is not uncommon for abused children to run to the abusive caretaker for comfort. Why would the child move in the direction of danger unless there is something instinctual or "programmed" in the child's gut that associates a caretaker with safety?

Whether you know it or not, you are terrified of causing trouble. However, the trouble I am talking about is actually referring to being assertive and honoring your true-self. Being assertive sounds easy, right? Think again.

In cases of severe abuse and neglect, the child's needs are so neglected they often do not know what their own needs are. Many children get scolded, grounded, laughed at, shunned, or abused for owning any unique want, feeling, or need. In such cases, the "gut" or instinct alerts the child that owning any of these aspects of the true-self is dangerous. In other words, it is trouble.

Because the child has very limited function in the part of the brain that deals with rational thought, a conclusion develops in the unconscious, which is: If I express my feelings or thoughts, I will cause trouble. If I cause trouble, I will be shunned. If I am shunned, I will not survive.

This adopted negative definition of troublemaking and survival become intertwined deep in the child's psyche, so much so that even as adults, people can literally feel panic at the very thought of standing up for themselves or expressing any feeling, thought, opinion, urge, or desire. It doesn't feel just scary, it feels terrifying. It's the kind of terror a child may feel when they are taken from their caretakers. It is because of this that it feels safe to live by accommodating others. Knowing what others want and accommodating them eliminates trouble. Except this is not so. The trouble lies within the accommodator, who is being neglected on a daily basis.

I work with people every day who cannot identify or express emotions, have no idea what they desire, pay no attention to dreams, and are ashamed of their urges. In some cases, they have never even held an opinion. To them, expressing themselves assertively is considered "trouble" and is consciously avoided at all costs. This is the life of an accommodator. It is common, and infinitely sad. Is this you? Do you fully know and honor those amazing qualities of your true-self? Do you feel free to assert and express yourself? Or does it feel awkward, uncomfortable, or dangerous? Take a minute and ask yourself how easy or difficult it is to:

- Set a limit by telling someone no to a request
- Express a feeling you know someone may dis-agree with
- Express an opinion of dissent
- Ask for something for yourself
- Do something for yourself
- Ask for help

Remember, an accommodating relational style is very convenient for the people you accommodate but is terribly inconvenient for you. As I will discuss in chapter 7, many people are not going to like the changes you are making as you start to stand up for yourself. This will perpetuate the sense that you are making trouble.

It is not uncommon for my clients to come into a session and report their loved ones had negative responses to their growth. This is because many of these people have experienced only accommodating from my clients. In other words, they have grown accustomed to getting their way. It is because of this that families also need intervention to understand why these changes are necessary, what to expect, and how to properly be supportive.

Bob's Story

I once worked with a newly retired business owner whom I will call Bob. He had sold his company for a handsome sum and was excited to start having fun in retirement. However, in time he developed a severe drinking problem. Through many discussions with Bob it became clear to me that the biggest change for him in retirement was the amount of time he spent with his wife. Bob adored his wife but due to the demands of his business the two had not spent a lot of alone time together for many years. When they were together, he often would go along with whatever she wanted because he either didn't care or was too tired to voice his opinion.

However, in retirement, Bob and his wife spent the majority of their time together. Although he was excited about this at first, he found himself unable to have opinions or express his desire to deviate from what she wanted to do. Bob and his wife had gotten too comfortable with her making all the decisions. Now, in retirement when he was supposed to be living it up, he found himself overwhelmed with everything she planned for him.

Rather than enjoying time with his wife, whom he loved dearly, he began to resent her. He began drinking, which caused even greater problems and distance. After learning about how his lack of honoring his own desires was directly related to his drinking, he became terrified at the thought of standing up for himself. He knew it would "cause trouble." In spite of his fear, he would often try to be assertive with her. Not surprisingly, she was not thrilled with her loss of power. During one session, Bob described his efforts this way:

"I have come to understand that her (his wife) definition of 'better' is me doing what she wants. However, through my treatment I have come to learn I have a very different definition of what it means to be better. For me to be better I need to start taking care of myself, standing up for myself, valuing my feelings, and valuing my needs. She says that is what she wants until I stand up for myself and all hell breaks loose."

In this case, Bob's wife saw his alcohol use as the only problem. She was happy being in control of his life and expected his accommodation. Anything that deviated from her control became a problem, and Bob felt like he was the cause. Like Bob's wife, many people do not understand the deeper underlying causes of addiction; they assume the only issue is the behavior of active addiction. They believe that if the drug behavior ends, the addict will relate to people the same way he or she always had when sober. This would not be a sign of progress and cannot happen. Sobriety must be more than absence of drugs to sustain a healthy recovery. You might be sober for a short time, but if you do not change how you relate to people, you will ultimately sink deeper into your addiction.

Learning to Be Assertive

As previously stated, troublemaking involves standing up for your feelings, needs, and desires. It also requires you to own your opinions and set healthy limits. It can be difficult but do not let fear overwhelm you. Start small. No effort is too small or meaningless. Here are some steps you can take to help you begin "making trouble" and stop your accommodating.

Setting Limits

Saying no, protecting your own physical or emotional space, or holding a strong opinion are examples of limit setting. Setting and maintaining limits can be challenging for anyone. For an accommodator, it is incredibly difficult because an accommodator doesn't want to be seen as a troublemaker. The accommodator has a heightened sensitivity to any cue that their own limit has inconvenienced others. When there are such cues, the accommodator is often riddled with anxiety and can instinctively resort to passivity. This is generally due to the false belief that setting a limit is bad, hurtful, or selfish.

Setting limits is not the same thing as aggression. When people are aggressive, they are interested in only their own position and want others to hold the same opinion or belief. However, when you assert limits, you are valuing and standing up for your position without forcing it onto anyone else. Moreover, you can still value another position while holding firm to yours.

Truthfully, setting limits does at times inconvenience people. That is okay. You are not responsible for getting others out of their dilemmas. Setting limits is not about intent to harm others. It is about identifying what personal space you want to protect and not allowing others to penetrate it.

Setting limits also involves protecting yourself by not getting absorbed into something you really do not want to be a part of. In other words, it requires saying no. Many people do not like to hear no and they will likely not like hearing it from you. However, this is their problem and issue to work through. You are an adult and have a right to set a limit and stand up for yourself. Challenge yourself to start setting limits in your life. These limits can be in relationships, work settings, with chemicals, food, shopping, and gambling. I can promise that the more you practice, the better you will feel and the more confidence you will develop.

To start, identify situations in which you would like to put up a limit. You can do this through journaling or making a list. Select one or two situations from your list and practice by actually saying no. You can even use imagery prior to any real interaction to help gain confidence. Here is a simple exercise with a positive rehearsal imagery:

Picture the actual place where you would like to set a limit. Picture all the details of the environment including the person or people with whom you will be setting the limit. Details are important to help you rehearse. Now picture yourself with a confident and strong physical posture. Picture confidence in your facial expressions as you interact. Bring up the incident you would like to say no to and imagine you are having the conversation.

With confidence in your facial expression, physical body, and voice, imagine saying no during the interaction. Now imagine yourself feeling solid, confident, and proud that you set a limit. Picture yourself confident with the knowledge that if your limit is not received well, it is not your problem. It is not because you are wrong or a bad person.

Practice that imagery as many times as you want. It can only strengthen your confidence in your ability to set a limit. Remember, setting limits is not only about keeping outside influences from influencing you, it's about sticking up for your own desires. Some examples of what you may say include:

- No I do not want to be _____.
- No I do not want to do _____.
- No I will not let you _____.
- No I can't do that for you_____.

Remember, some people will not like your newfound assertiveness. Be persistent anyway. If you back down, you are teaching others that if only they push hard enough, you will give in to them. Accommodating others is what brought you problems in the first place.

If you find you need help setting limits, seek support from friends or loved ones. If that fails, seek professional help (counseling or support groups) to get the support you deserve.

Expressing Yourself

Getting in touch with what you need or feel is not enough. You need to stand up for your true-self. In doing so, you are allowing yourself to experience and express emotions, take care of your needs, and follow your dreams and desires. Much like when setting a limit, you will have some hesitancy in expressing yourself.

Troublemaking involves standing up for your feelings, needs, and desires. It also requires you to own your opinions and set healthy limits. It can be difficult, but do not let fear overwhelm you. Start small. No effort is to small or meaningless.

You may think you are hurting others, being aggressive, or overreacting. People around you may suggest you are being selfish or unfair. You need to silence your inner critic and learn not to absorb what others are attempting to make you believe. You have a right to state your feelings. You have a right to get your needs met. You have a right to follow your dreams. If others decide to get in the way, it's time to move them out of the way.

As part of expressing yourself, remember to set good limits. Use your limit setting to put space between you and those who are not willing to support your growth. You have spent your lifetime considering what others want or need. It's time to extend that same courtesy to yourself. You will need to push through the discomfort and anxiety and begin to be assertive, express your feelings, and request things from others.

Being assertive involves being direct with your communication. You can no longer use body language, sarcasm, or any other passive methods to communicate.

You will have to speak your mind in a firm and direct way. This includes asserting your thoughts, opinions, feelings, and needs. It requires you to know what your position is on topics and issues—from what you would like to eat to a political or religious stance. You have to be willing to state your opinion or feeling and stand firm.

Being assertive is not about breaking down someone else or trying to win. It's about learning how to be healthy and root for yourself as well as for others in your life. After all, that is what true emotional intimacy is. It's about all of us caring about what each other feels, needs, and wants. We are all facing the same challenge, which is to negotiate a healthy life and relationships.

Identifying and expressing your feelings does take a lot of courage, especially if this has not been a rewarding experience for you in the past. It can seem easier to just keep your feelings to yourself. But, as previously discussed, this is not healthy and opens the door for many problems because feelings will take a shadow form. You will need to step outside of your comfort zone and own your feelings. Your feelings are valid and you have a right to express them. Try to be assertive rather than aggressive when you are communicating how you feel. You can do this by using "I statements" such as, "I feel upset" or "I feel disappointed." There doesn't have to be an identified reason. You can simply state how you feel.

Consider what your expectations are for being expressive. Your goal must be to stand up for yourself. If you have expectations about how your expression will be received, it may discourage you. You are the one committing to changes. If others in your life have not also committed, you can expect they will respond in the same manner in which they always have. If your feelings are not acknowledged or validated, it can be extremely painful. In these times, it is important to remind yourself of why you are trying to make changes. Moreover, try to understand that others may not be ready or able to support you in the way in which you need it.

Over time, you will discover the profound value in true-self and see things more objectively. The more you are able to continue working on valuing yourself and expressing your true-self, the easier it will be to identify others who do or do not have your best interest at heart. When this happens, you may decide to limit your time with or even terminate relationships with people who are not willing to acknowledge or value you.

Telling Others What You Need

Expressing yourself also involves asking things of other people. I am not referring to money or any material things that money can buy. What you need to ask of others is that they give you time, give you acknowledgement, and respect your boundaries.

By time, I mean patience as you learn how to be healthy and how to engage in new relational dynamics. Sometimes this means time in a more structured environment like a therapeutic setting. Essentially, you are asking loved ones to be a part of the healing process. This is not burdening them. Someone who truly cares about you will sacrifice their time to help you become healthy.

You also need to ask that people acknowledge your feelings and opinions. This is not saying they have to agree with everything. It is requesting that they try to understand you and acknowledge your feelings are real and important.

You will also need to stand firm on your limits and boundaries and ask that others respect them. Maybe your boundary is not being yelled at or told what to do. Or maybe it's not wanting to spend time with a family member who has insulted, used, or abused you. In these cases, you are asking that loved ones do not yell at you or treat you like a child. You are asking loved ones to not use emotional manipulation to guilt you into being around someone who makes you uncomfortable. You are asking people to respect you and your boundaries.

Again, the more you practice, the easier it will be to identify who in your life is healthy for you and who is destructive. As you can probably assume, the specific action steps to practice expressing yourself are limitless. In my practice, my clients have reported practicing saying no to agreeing to someone else's restaurant choice, giving money when asked for it, or giving up their time if they'd prefer not to. I have also seen clients glowing with pride after saying yes to almost anything they want or need.

Being assertive is not about breaking down someone else or trying to win. It is about learning how to be healthy and root for yourself as well as for others in your life.

Because there is a natural drive to set limits and take care of the true-self, when people in recovery finally do so they feel so good they never want to go back to the old accommodating relational style. Moreover, since they are in a better position to identify and eliminate destructive people, they have enhanced personal relationships. Research has shown time after time that meaningful healthy relationships are essential to maintaining sobriety.

Summary

People often have a strange love–hate relationship with troublemaking. However, now you have learned how to redefine troublemaking as the ability to stand up for yourself. You do this by knowing and understanding your desires, needs, feelings, and boundaries. Once you can honor your true-self, you can begin to be assertive with others. It can be scary, but if you challenge yourself to be assertive with your true-self, I promise you that it will pay off.

Part III

Unlikely Foes:
Family, Loved Ones,
and Self-Help Groups

7

Family and Loved Ones

*Notice the people who are happy for your happiness,
and sad for your sadness. They're the ones who deserve
special places in your heart.*
—Lisa Marie Schiffner, social media celebrity

Family and other loved ones are of great importance in our lives. Our experiences with our family and loved ones can leave us feeling anywhere between greatly loved or deeply betrayed. Because you are going to be working on asserting yourself, your interactions with family and loved ones will change. I want you to be fully prepared for what you may experience in your relationships during this process of growth. This will be not only how your family and loved ones relate to you, but also your own responsibility in how you relate to them.

The Benefits of Healthy Relationships

During my first psychology class in college, I remember learning about research done on lab rats involving cocaine. Researchers put rats into an isolated cage and put two separate drop feeders in the space. One of the feeders supplied food, the other cocaine. It was discovered that once the rats got a taste of cocaine, they had no interest in food or anything else. The rats would seemingly prefer starvation rather than to give up cocaine. I can still hear my professor proclaim that drugs are so dangerous that rats would rather die than live without them.

It wasn't until later I learned this was only a part of the story. It turns out that in the late 1970s a Canadian psychologist named Bruce Alexander challenged the study. Dr. Alexander suggested that since the rats studied were in isolation, perhaps they had miserable lives which made a chemical's effect very desirable. So, Dr. Alexander created Rat Park, which was a massive living and playing space for the rats. He filled it with toys, wheels, balls, food, and most importantly, other rats. In this space, rats had access to everything a rat could want; they were able to play together, and they were able to mate.

Dr. Alexander also supplied the rats water laced with morphine. However, in Rat Park, something very different happened from the previous rat cocaine studies. Some of the rats actually did use and enjoy the chemical. However, the overwhelming majority of the rats were not interested because they were enjoying their lives in Rat Park.

There have been other studies like this one by Dr. Alexander, with similar results. Many of these researchers have concluded that the opposite of addiction is not sobriety. The opposite of addiction is a good quality of life and genuine, healthy relationships. Of course, any discussion on significant relationships involves our first social connections, our family.

Addiction Affects the Entire Family

There is no way through addiction without pain for the entire family. Too often, people who are addicted get labeled or targeted as the problem. However, the work to achieve healthy, supportive relationships extends beyond the addict themselves. The other half of the work belongs to those family members and loved ones the addicted person interacts with.

Early in my career I discontinued my work with children because I was so saddened by the number of parents who took no ownership in the problems their children were facing. The child may have had the most visible problem, but more often than not, the behavior was just a symptom of a family issue.

People do not exist in a vacuum. For every chemically addicted person I have worked with, there is at least one person who is in a conspiracy with them to keep the addiction alive. Many of these coconspirators have no idea they are causing harm. In fact, they may actually believe they are helping.

Sometimes even well-intended people can negatively impact your recovery. Don't be afraid to use your assertiveness to set limits with family and loved ones unwilling to allow you to be your true-self. The support that will help you the most will be from those people who work with you and honor your true-self just as you are learning to.

Part of the reason people may not know they may be harming you is because you are too accommodating. Unless you are a mind reader, it is impossible to know how you impact someone if they do not tell you. Just as others need to understand their role in maintaining a healthy relationship with you, you must also understand yours.

An example of accommodation may look something like this. A friend or family member asks in a passive or manipulative way for something from you. To not make trouble, you accommodate their request. You do this whether you want to or not. This results in a dynamic in which the person asking you for something gets what he or she wants, and you do not. This works out great for the people who are consistently being accommodated, but not so great for you. Moreover, since there is no external dissent or conflict, the people you accommodate do not recognize a problem. There is, however, conflict internally for you, so much so that you will develop resentments and may even blame your support family and friends for being so "controlling."

The problem, of course, is that you are also very much responsible for this relational dynamic. As I stated previously, this accommodating relational style developed in childhood out of necessity. However, you are no longer a child. At some point, you need to understand that as an adult you have a right to stand up for yourself. This includes acknowledging your feelings, needs, and desires. As an adult, you can say no when necessary and yes when appropriate.

I am constantly asking clients to own the fact that they have let others walk all over them. I will ask the same of you. Take responsibility for choosing to swallow your needs and feelings rather than express them. Own that you have a hard time setting limits. In doing so, you give yourself power. If you own the choice of not standing up for yourself, you can make the choice to do so. It is your responsibility to make that choice. The more you honor your true-self, the easier this will feel.

Your New Dilemma:
Some People Will Not Like the "New You"

Expressing yourself in a healthy way will likely be new for you. Because this is a new behavior and a change to the relational dynamic, you also need to be aware that the people around you may not like it. This is why it is very important that your family and loved ones understand how they may be contributing to your addiction. In other words, loved ones need to understand their role in the accommodating relationship and how it perpetuates addiction.

Family members and close friends are all affected by one's addiction. Supportive family relationships help in the recovery process.

Family, Friends, and the Changing You

Your family and loved ones may be shocked or even angry that you are being assertive. After all, they are used to getting their way. This is why it is important that your supportive loved ones are willing to change as well. Like you, they need to take responsibility for their contribution to the accommodating relationship. This includes a willingness to own past or present usage of manipulation or other tactics to try and get their way. They must be willing to allow you to use your personal power to honor your true-self.

In my experience, it is not uncommon for some of this information to be taken as insulting to those who are trying to support you. Loved ones may only hear that they are "causing" the addiction by taking advantage of you—the accommodator. In fairness, if they are being accommodated, how could they know there is a problem if you didn't tell them? Nevertheless, your supportive loved ones need to understand that your intent is not to insult them when you are being assertive. If they can't understand this, it could possibly be just another manipulation tactic to make you feel less comfortable about standing up for yourself. This is serious "gut-check" time. Oftentimes, family members and loved ones may find themselves in therapy to help them adapt to the changes in the relationship. This can be quite helpful and necessary. Everyone has to understand what needs to happen, own their responsibility, and demonstrate willingness to change.

After your family and loved ones allow you to be your true-self, own their responsibility, and demonstrate willingness to change, they are in a position to be fully supportive. This includes not only listening, but asking about, valuing, and encouraging your feelings, opinions, needs, and desires. In doing so, family members and loved ones must to be willing to give up getting their way at times. They have to be willing to give space if needed, give up things they want, and be okay hearing "no." The relationship can no longer exist in its previous form. All parties involved need to learn negotiating skills.

When you try to negotiate a new relational style, you will get resistance. Even well-intended family members and loved ones who may initially love the idea of being supportive can easily fall back to old relational patterns. When this happens, you will experience more anxiety and again become hesitant to stand up for yourself. It is very important that you continue to be assertive in spite of this.

If you are continually met with resistance, you will be faced with decisions that can have profound consequences. One decision is to fall back on the "easier," more comfortable approach of accommodating. I cannot overstate how important it is to not do this. Any accommodation in the early stages of sobriety is reinforcement to those who are demanding of you. This will ultimately lead back to, and strengthen, the pattern you are trying to change. If you fall into this trap, relapse becomes inevitable.

Cutting Relationships: The Ultimate Limit

Sometimes, another profoundly painful decision is whether or not to cut ties with the relationship. You need to decide whether a relationship is destructive for you. As I have suggested, the more you express yourself, the easier it will be to identify those who have no interest in your well-being. Be aware that even when you understand it is healthy for you to exit a relationship, the decision carries sadness, stress, anxiety, even anger.

You need to prepare for the possibility that some of your family and loved ones are not willing to change. You may also need to keep a distance from people in an effort to eliminate destructive relationships. You may find that you try to be assertive and get nothing in return. It is up to you to continue to assert yourself and confidently require others to treat you appropriately. If people are not respecting this, you may need to keep your distance from the relationship altogether.

Keeping your distance is not the same thing as avoidance. Sometimes people will withdraw from others to avoid having to hold them accountable. It can feel easier or safer to just stay away. However, that carries with it a sense of powerlessness and passivity. You never get the chance to stand up for yourself. Therefore, you may remain somewhat accommodating. Those in your life never have to hear or be faced with the discomfort of how you feel. Also, with avoidance, you can rob yourself of gaining confidence in your ability to command dignity and respect.

The Best Support Systems Work with You

The greatest successes I have seen come from a combination of my clients practicing being assertive and family members encouraging it. Sometimes clients come to me and state that their parents, spouses, or friends actually say, "You are supposed to be telling me what you want." That is the kind of support and encouragement that is needed. Unfortunately, this is not always the case. However, I am convinced there are many people out there who are willing to provide you with the love and support you deserve. As you get more secure in your own value, you will recruit quality people into your life and sustain healthy relationships.

Summary

Our families and loved ones are of great importance to us. However, supportive people are still human and humans are not perfect. We all make mistakes. The human element cannot be removed from your recovery. You now know that sometimes even well-intended people can negatively impact your recovery. Don't be afraid to use your assertiveness to set limits with family or loved ones unwilling to allow you to be your true-self. Sometimes, this even requires cutting off relationships. The support that will help you the most will be from those people who work with you and honor your true-self just as you are learning to.

8

Self-Help Groups

Whoever fights monsters should see to it that in the process he does not become a monster.

—Friedrich Nietzsche, philosopher

Since its first meeting in the late 1930s, Alcoholics Anonymous (AA) has been a popular form of treatment for alcoholics. Many of my clients view its text, known as the Big Book, as the second most important book in human history behind only the Bible. Moreover, the majority of these clients have been taught that the twelve-step process of AA is the only method that can truly save them from an inevitable alcohol-related death.

Other self-help groups have developed since AA began that follow a similar twelve-step approach. These include, but are not limited to, Narcotics Anonymous (NA), Gamblers Anonymous (GA), Sex Addicts Anonymous (SAA), and Overeaters Anonymous (OA) to name a few. These programs offer sometimes irreplaceable resources to help someone radically transform their life. Some of the potential benefits include: nonjudgmental peer support, accountability, opportunities to learn from others, opportunities to talk openly, and referrals to other services. With all of these healthful benefits, it is no wonder why self-help groups have helped contribute to the ongoing success of many people in their recovery.

Are Self-Help Groups Right for You?

Although I could go on at length, this chapter is not dedicated to the numerous payoffs of self-help group participation. Rather, I want to shed light on the potential harm of working with a self-help group. Believe it or not, there is a dark side to self-help groups that is rarely, if ever, spoken about by professionals. I know about this "dark side" because over the past ten years I have often heard from my clients about damaging experiences they have had in these groups. Many of these clients were once strongly encouraged by the potential benefits of participating in a self-help group. However, by experiencing some of the issues I will discuss, they have since sworn off self-help groups altogether.

If you are in a group that does not value your feelings, opinions, or subjective experiences, find a group that will. It's okay to continue exploring until you find a group that honors who you are.

One thing I want to make clear is that I have no problems with the actual "twelve steps" of any self-help group. The "steps" are guiding principles that are designed to help recovery. The term "step-work" describes when someone is applying one or more of these steps to their life. Most of the actual step-work can be very useful and, if done properly, healing. What the actual step-work can't do is make sure the individuals in these groups are conducting themselves properly. Just because you are in a group with guiding principles that are based on acceptance, support, and mutual respect, there is no guarantee those values will be practiced by all its members. The damage I am referring to exists outside the text and twelve steps. Rather, it is in the relational dynamics of the group itself.

My hope is that you can learn to recognize, and avoid, these damaging practices. This will help you own the power of deciding which groups are healthy for you

It's difficult to recover alone from addiction. Support groups can have a strong impact on emotional healing.

and which you should avoid, thus dramatically increasing the chances you will receive all the potential benefits of self-help group participation highlighted earlier.

In this book I have argued that anger, healthy selfishness, and troublemaking are necessary in order to heal from addiction. I use the word "heal" because healing is very different from changing behavior to appear healthy. I have suggested the accommodating relational style is developed from early relational experiences and is the blueprint for addiction. Furthermore, I argue that if your family and loved ones do not understand what you need or what is required for lasting change, they will resume their role of demanding to be accommodated. The same can be true for those whom you will interact with in a self-help group.

As mentioned earlier, what is needed in recovery is new relational dynamics with the people you interact with. Those in recovery need supportive people who attempt to acknowledge, accept, and allow them to be unique individuals. New ideas, thoughts, and feelings should be recognized as valuable and should be encouraged. This is a chance for the person in recovery to be fully accepted, maybe for the first time in their life. Any deviation from this acceptance is a replication of early experiences and is very damaging.

Over the years, I have heard my clients discuss in detail having experienced some of the issues I am going to warn you about while participating in a self-help group. Believe it or not, like it or not, bad practice is a reality. I want you to be able to spot these behaviors and recognize them as destructive. Moreover, I want to give you permission to either stand up for yourself or walk away if necessary. There are two damaging experiences I hear about most often: the concept of being seen and not heard and the concept of rock bottom.

Seen and Not Heard

I have listened to the testimonials of many people after their first experience with a self-help group. I am acutely aware that it is not uncommon for a new member of a group to be told to sit down, listen, and learn. In some cases, it is not uncommon for the new members to even be criticized if they offer opinions, being told "your best thinking got you here," implying an addict cannot possibly think well.

These two messages together—"just listen to what I am saying," and "you do not have anything to offer"—is an exact replication of the earlier accommodating relational experiences. As one former client, a thirty-four-year-old graduate student, put it, "It's like if you don't agree with every little thing, there is something wrong with you. Basically, I don't know anything so I should just shut up. Reminds me of home."

Of course, it is appropriate that you acknowledge and are ready to respect the rules of any group you are joining. However, it is often not the core principles of these groups that participants are being asked to respect and accommodate. Rather, new members are being required to accommodate the opinions and wants of fellow peers. This can be particularly true in a sponsor/sponsee relationship.

A sponsor can easily fall into the trap of "I know best so listen to me." Sometimes, the sponsor may actually cut off the sponsee if there is not total compliance. In more extreme cases, a sponsor may encourage other members of the group to do the same. Many of these opinions stem from an overall belief that a person in recovery has to surrender all that they are and all that they believe to be true. These beliefs are likely a misinterpretation of the actual step-work involved.

I guarantee that there are good people who lead and participate in self-help groups or other groups that are designed to offer a quality, healing experience. You just have to be able to spot an abusive situation and be willing to leave in order to find a healthy one.

For example, in many self-help groups, steps one and two have to do with powerlessness and acceptance of a power greater than self, which is an essential aid in recovery. However, interpreting this as a complete surrender to everything is a mistake. First, it puts limits on the encouragement of owning your true-self. If you really don't know anything, then why would you look internally to get answers? Moreover, if you give away all your power, how will you ever discover yours? As I stated earlier, the other, equally disturbing, issue is that it creates an environment that demands compliance. The underlying message is often heard as: you have no power and do not know anything, so give up your power to me and listen to my advice.

In this kind of environment, there is no room for the uniqueness of an individual and no value given to the feelings, thoughts, urges, or opinions of the person. On the contrary, many are told that their feelings are wrong, their thoughts are flawed, and their urges are dangerous. Any kind of dissent from the group's thoughts or opinions can be met with criticism or accusations of denial. These dynamics are incredibly damaging for two reasons. First, a new member could recognize them as abusive and exit the program altogether, carrying the assumption that every group is the same. Secondly, a new member could fall back into the role of accommodator, behaving accordingly but never developing the skills to make internal changes.

There is great danger in accommodating messages that say you know nothing, that you must sit and be silent until you are spoken to, that you must just listen and learn. This is a complete replication of the accommodating relational style. It's destructive, unhealthy, unloving, and will not create an environment in which healing can take place. I cannot imagine a worse treatment scenario than being "treated" for an illness with the same poison that made one sick.

Rock Bottom

The term "rock bottom" is often used in AA to describe a turning point for a chemically addicted person. The idea is that when addiction has brought the person to the lowest point in their life (rock bottom), they will be distressed enough to make changes. Without a rock bottom experience, the person is not fully aware of the extent of their problem.

This idea, though true for some, is potentially damaging to some group members. Many chemically addicted people have been shamed, abused, and neglected for many years. Their accommodating relational style has left them with no self-value, self-respect, or self-confidence. When they finally make a decision to enter treatment, it can be extremely anxiety-provoking.

Now suppose this anxious person has a significant problem but has never experienced catastrophic consequences (rock bottom). If they do not conform to the ideas and opinions of the group members, what may happen? Often, these people are told they are not ready to change or have yet to experience rock bottom.

This message is similar to those interwoven into the accommodating relationship. The implied message is that you must see things how we see them or you are not ready to be included (a demand for accommodation). Furthermore, these messages can be interpreted as you are not sick enough because you have not hit the lowest point. This is not only presumptuous, it totally disregards and devalues the subjective experience of the individual.

Even though newcomers to a group may be in intense emotional pain, many of them are told they are not ready because they need to be sicker or suffer more. Imagine how helpless and alone this would feel for someone who has already felt neglected their entire life. As one former client, a sixty-year-old barber, put it, "So here I am finally getting the balls to go and expose myself to the world. My whole damn life I feel like a piece of (expletive)… and these people tell me I'm not ready because I haven't had enough happen to me. So I'm not even good enough for treatment I guess."

Developing Healthy, New Relationships

People in recovery need to experience new relational dynamics. New and healthy relationships must invite and encourage uniqueness, not demand compliance. Encouraging uniqueness involves accepting, not rejecting, the emergence of one's true-self. In other words, a healthy group and/or sponsor will care about what you have to offer and understand you are not there to please them or make them feel smart or valuable. They will take you seriously no matter where you are in your recovery. They will honor your feelings, thoughts, and needs. When you find this, you will not have to worry about not being good enough (sick enough), or being accepted only if you accommodate.

If you are exploring self-help groups, or any group, and recognize these patterns, I have something to tell you. If you are in a group that does not value your feelings, opinions, or subjective experiences, find a group that will. It is okay to continue exploring until you find a group that honors who you are. It is healthy to have your own opinions or thoughts on what is best for you. You can empower yourself to continue looking until you find the right support system that will help foster your own growth by empowering you to discover your own unique voice.

I guarantee that there are good people who lead and participate in self-help groups or other groups that are designed to offer a quality, healing experience. You just have to be able to spot an abusive situation and be willing to leave in order find a healthy one.

Summary

Alcoholics Anonymous and self-help groups like it have been around since the 1930s. Nobody can doubt these groups have helped countless people since that time. The principles or "steps" are solid in theory. This does not always mean that all self-help groups are practiced the same way or even appropriately. Be aware of destructive messages such as, "you must listen and not talk," "your best thinking got you here," or "you are not sick enough—you must hit rock bottom." These messages are destructive and replicate many of the problems you have had in relationships your entire life. Be strong and use your assertiveness to put up firm limits in order to find the group that works for you, a group that will honor your feelings, thoughts, opinions, and struggles.

9

The Art of Balance

Life is a balance of holding on, letting go, and knowing when to do which of the two.

—Unknown

At the beginning of this book, I discussed how the "blueprint" for addictive disorders develops. I later offered what I believe to be the three key tools (anger, self-care, and troublemaking) to conquer such addictions. Now, I would like to help further prepare you for actually applying these strategies. It will not be easy. Please keep in mind that your interaction style has been running for a long time. Challenging these ingrained patterns will feel odd, even dangerous. Don't be surprised if you find yourself being pulled back into what is familiar.

Change Is Not Easy

Change, even healthy change, can be very anxiety-provoking. Additionally, all change is difficult. If you disagree, try brushing your teeth tonight with your nondominant hand. You will find your brain begging you to take the easier, more familiar route of using your dominate hand. Stress, difficulty, fatigue, and anxiety all have the potential to divert you from change of any kind. This difficulty often results in short-term attempts at minor changes. Rarely do these efforts result in any profound long-term changes. Often, we tell ourselves it's just too hard! However, if you have reasonable expectations, you can put things into perspective and change will feel more manageable.

Be Willing to Do the Work

Meaningful and lasting change comes from persistence, hard work, discipline, and a great deal of discomfort. It involves taking healthy risks in order to challenge yourself, your history, your perspective, and your relationships. There are no shortcuts and no methods for eliminating the discomfort that comes with any kind of growth. Consider this: a person may want to be built like a bodybuilder and may even take initiative to develop the "perfect" workout plan. However, if this person does not show up at the gym and go through the pain of pushing their muscles to the max, there is no growth. I think you would find throughout all areas of life that little pain equals little reward.

This will be some of the hardest work you will ever do, and it will impact your relationship with yourself and others. At times, it will feel aggressive, inappropriate, or even threatening. Following through can take more than you are willing to give. However, if you are willing to persevere, you will not be dissatisfied.

Achieving Balance

Changing your ingrained relational patterns requires that you learn to master the balancing act between your ego and its shadow. Since accommodating others creates a significant psychological imbalance, you need to reach an equilibrium in your psyche.

Extremes of anything will disrupt balance and, in turn, have the potential to cause problems. In America, we seem to live an extreme culture. We supersize everything, maximize credit cards, and are entertained by extreme behavior. These extremes, unfortunately, often carry with

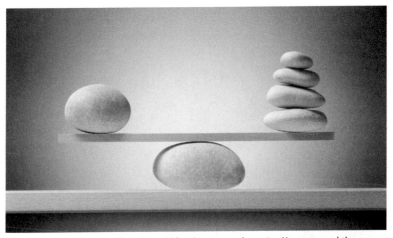

Learning to live an emotionally balanced life takes time and practice. You can speed the process with solid emotional support such as that from a therapist.

them extreme consequences. Extreme consumption of processed sugar and fatty foods results in extremely poor health. Extreme overspending results in extreme financial debt. Extreme work habits results in burnout. And, as I have argued throughout this book, extreme accommodating leads to extreme self-neglect, which leads to addiction.

How does one restore this psychological balance that I am referring to? Let me start by giving you a simple metaphor to help illustrate how to reach the balance of healthy self-care. Consider a pendulum swinging from left to right—left being extreme accommodation (caring only for others) and right being extreme narcissism (caring only for self). The center, or balance, represents healthy self-care (caring for self and others). Now, it is your task to make sure the pendulum rests still in the center without putting it there with your hand. How would you do this? Without forcing it to the center, your only option is to drop the pendulum and let it swing to the opposite side, then back again and again until it finds its own balance in the center.

To make the changes you want, you must push yourself to experience the direct opposite of accommodating. In other words, you must be overly aggressive with self-care, anger, and troublemaking. In doing so, you will feel the negative aspects of these characteristics. You may have to be aggressive, find yourself easily irritated, and have increased friction in personal and social relationships. The reason for this is you are learning a whole new way to interact with the world. It will be a little clumsy and frustrating at first.

You are not aiming to end up living in this extreme. Over time, you will learn what does and does not work for you. It will happen through your own experience, on your own power, and at your own pace. Just like the pendulum, you will rock back and forth trying to find a balance that is right for you. It is there, in the balance, where you will discover healthy anger expression, self-care, and troublemaking.

Achieving balance in this way is difficult work and takes healthy risks and support to accomplish. The accommodating response is so ingrained in the psyche that if you inch along too cautiously you will quickly be pulled back to behaving the way you always have. Think of a frigid pool on a cool day. If you just dip your toe in, your instincts are likely going to deter you from swimming. However, if you jump in, you are forced to deal with the discomfort until your body temperature adjusts. At that point, it becomes actually more comfortable to be in the pool than out in the cool air.

Amanda's Story

One of my clients, whom I will refer to as Amanda, is a thirty-nine-year-old wife and stay-at-home mom. Amanda had tears of joy while telling me about finding her balance. "I used to take care of everyone. Looking back, I can't believe how many people relied on me. Even people at church asked favors constantly, mostly because they knew I would say yes. At the end of the day, I was just so tired. The only thing I wanted to do was eat and watch TV. Drinking totally numbed me out. I really feel good about where I am now. I mean, at first I felt like a total bitch. And I probably was being mean. I just couldn't figure it out right away."

In time you will discover your balance. It will eventually feel so good that you will never want to go back to accommodating. You will understand, know, and feel healthy anger expression, self-care, and troublemaking. In doing so, you will master the skill of honoring and expressing your true-self. When you live this way, the unconscious need for any chemical abuse ceases to exist.

Amanda continued, "I had no experience telling others what I really wanted. But I feel like now I can just say no to people. It doesn't have to be harsh. If people can't handle a no from me, it's not really my problem. It's crazy how much things have changed; it feels so amazing to take care of me! I am not going back. When I set limits with everyone else in my life, I make room for healthy meal planning, exercise, and some kind of social life. I really don't even think about drinking."

Just like Amanda and many others, you can adjust. You have experienced the problems of accommodating. By experimenting with anger, healthy selfishness, and troublemaking you will experience some problems with these skills as well. However, in time you will discover your balance. It will eventually feel so good that you will never want to go back to accommodating. You will understand, know, and feel healthy anger expression, self-care, and troublemaking. In doing so, you will master the skill of honoring and expressing your true-self. When you live this way, the unconscious need for any chemical abuse ceases to exist.

Summary

Experiencing too much of any extreme is not healthy. You can work to achieve the balance that is healthy for you. This can require you to experience an exaggerated version of what you want to get. Sometimes people who are not very social need to be overly social in order to reach what social balance is right for them. In your case, you will have to be overly assertive, maybe even aggressive, with your true-self. It's then you will learn what works and what doesn't. Somewhere in between the extremes you will find your perfect balance.

In Conclusion

Why not go out on a limb?
Isn't that where the fruit is?
—Frank Scully, American journalist

Too many people are in a constant state of emotional turmoil ruminating over the past or focusing on present external stressors. This can be especially true for those suffering from addiction. Maybe you are, or have been, one of these people. Right now, you have an opportunity to challenge your perspective and approach recovery in an entirely new way. Go out on a limb! You can begin living your life in a way that honors who you are. The intention of the book is to help you do just that! It is my hope that what you learned will challenge you to consider developing the characteristics I believe are essential to reach optimal health and recovery.

It is too easy to fall into the trap of labeling ourselves and others as "bad" or "good" based on behavior. As I have said, in the case of addicted behavior, these labels are misleading. Don't continue to fall into this trap. You can separate what you do from who you are. You can give full acknowledgement to your true-self. You can experience what it feels like to actually use anger, self-care, and troublemaking to your advantage. You, and only you, have the power to do so.

You will be successful when you honor and empower your true-self. Your true-self carries your rawest emotions, sweetest desires, deepest dreams, and intense urges. You do not have to work on developing these valuable components of your true-self. You were born with them. However, people rejected them, and you have learned to suppress them. Now is the time to empower your true-self in order to conquer addiction. Now is the time to utilize anger, self-care, and troublemaking to achieve recovery. These components of the true-self were designed to protect you. Harness the energy from these gifts and experience the benefit of healthy relationships, strong boundaries, self-security, and sustained sobriety.

With my own two eyes I have witnessed how anger, self-care, and troublemaking can transform the recovery process. As I stated, at times it will be incredibly difficult. You will no doubt find yourself being pulled back to familiar relational patterns. If you continue to live your life in that way, you will find yourself in the same repetitive cycle. This will certainly leave you feeling frustrated and exhausted. You will be looking for answers in the same old places. You may even find yourself being asked by a therapist what you are willing to do differently. Just like my client Danielle, in chapter 1, you may respond with, "Whatcha got?"

The good news is you do not have to revert back to a life of accommodation. You can push through the obstacles. The tools outlined in this book will help you! With anger, self-care, and troublemaking now being utilized to your advantage, you are equipped to end your addiction once and for all!

Appendix

Treatment Programs

Because you have read this book, I know that the chances are good that you, or someone you care about, is struggling with an addiction. Maybe this book is your first attempt at learning something about addiction.

I also know that admitting you may have a problem can be difficult and even scary. Moreover, making the decision to enter an actual treatment program can be terrifying. I want you to know that treatment for addiction does not have to be monumentally difficult or exceedingly terrifying.

There are many different treatment options that can help manage the difficulty and ease the anxiety of recovery. In this Appendix, I would like to give you a brief summary of the types of options for treatment.

Medication-Assisted Therapy (MAT)

In the last decade, drugs have become available to treat addiction. Known as medication-assisted therapy, these drugs help individuals get off opioids and can help prevent relapse. Methadone, buprenorphine, naltrexone, and naloxone *(Narcan)* are the most common.

Methadone

Methadone is a full opiate agonist. This means that methadone works in the brain's reward center in the same way other opiates such as heroin, morphine, codeine, and hydrocodone do. Clients who take methadone tend to have less craving for and use less heroin or other opioids of abuse. Detoxification or acute withdrawal is not necessary in order to begin methadone treatment. Methadone must be taken under the supervision of a licensed doctor. Methadone treatment usually begins by receiving the proper dosage at a licensed clinic. However, once stabilized, the medication can be taken at home like other prescription medications. Methadone treatment is usually used in combination with talk therapy.

Buprenorphine

Buprenorphine is another drug used to help people get off opioids. Sold under the brand name *Suboxone* (and others), buprenorphine is considered an opiate partial agonist. This means that the drug will provide a euphoric effect but it is weaker than other opiate drugs. People taking buprenorphine tend to have fewer cravings for opioid drugs. Unlike methadone treatment, clients seeking buprenorphine must be in the early stages of opioid withdrawal before taking the first dose. Buprenorphine must be taken under the supervision of a licensed doctor, trained to prescribe the drug.

Naltrexone

Naltrexone is used to treat alcohol and opioid dependence. It helps prevent relapse by reducing cravings. Naltrexone is an opiate antagonist. Unlike methadone and buprenorphine, rather than occupying opiate receptors in the brain, naltrexone blocks them. Therefore, if an opiate drug is taken while taking naltrexone, there is no euphoric effect. Naltrexone can only be used after a person has fully detoxified from opiates. People taking naltrexone tend to have less cravings for opioids and are less likely to relapse. Although methadone and buprenorphine treat opiate users only, naltrexone is used to treat alcohol abuse and dependence. It does so by blocking the euphoric effects of alcohol. Naltrexone can be prescribed by any health care provider who is licensed to prescribe medication.

Naloxone (Narcan)

Naloxone, also known as *Narcan,* can save the life of someone who has overdosed on opioids. Naloxone works by

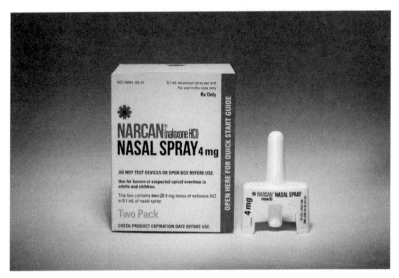

Narcan can save a life. A nasal spray, it is available without a prescription at virtually all drug stores in the United States.

reversing the lethal effects to the central nervous system and the respiratory system caused by an overdose of opiates.

According to the World Health Organization (WHO), the "opioid overdose triad" is a combination of three signs and symptoms associated with opioid overdose. The three symptoms are:

- Pinpoint pupils
- Unconsciousness
- Respiratory depression (slow and shallow breathing)

How to Use Narcan. Narcan is given as a nasal spray. The website narcan.com offers a quick guide for opioid overdose responders. The guide offers four steps in administering the nasal spray. The steps are:

1. Remove the nasal spray from the box and peel the tab with the circle to open the nasal spray.
2. Hold the nasal spray with your thumb on the bottom of the plunger and your first and middle fingers on either side of the nozzle.

3. Gently insert tip of the nozzle into either nostril. If necessary, gently tilt the head back and provide support under the neck with your other hand.

4. Press the plunger firmly to give the dose of *Narcan* nasal spray and remove the nozzle from the nostril.

Narcan is relatively easy to get and available without a prescription at most pharmacies in the United States.

Who May Need Narcan? If you are addicted to opioid drugs, you should carry *Narcan*. Let those around you know how to use it and where you keep it. It's also a good idea for people with loved ones who struggle with opioid addiction to carry *Narcan*. Others who should have *Narcan* available include those who have used opioids for long-term chronic pain as well as those who take opioids in combination with sleep medications. Also, those with medical conditions such as depression, HIV, and lung or liver disease should have access to *Narcan*. Emergency responders and health care providers should carry *Narcan* also. For more information, visit: narcan. com

Medical Detoxification

Medical detoxification is a medically supervised process that prepares an individual for treatment. Individuals who have long-term addictions typically face painful withdrawal symptoms when they come off drugs or alcohol. In severe cases, the withdrawal can be fatal. In a detox facility an individual can be safely stabilized by medical staff in preparation for treatment.

Withdrawal symptoms from alcohol may include:

- Shaky hands
- Nausea
- Vomiting
- Insomnia
- Sweating

More serious alcohol withdrawal symptoms include:

- Hallucinations
- Seizures
- Confusion

- Fever
- Racing heart
- High blood pressure
- Death

Although the effects of opioid withdrawal are not fatal, it can often feel so horrible, you may think it's fatal. Some people describe such withdrawal as a terrible case of influenza. Common opioid withdrawal symptoms include:

- Anxiety
- Restlessness/Restless legs
- Insomnia
- Body aches
- Sweating
- Vomiting and diarrhea
- Fever
- Rapid heartbeat and rapid breathing
- Hallucinations
- Seizures

Mild benzodiazepine withdrawal symptoms include:

- Sleep disturbances
- Increased tension
- Anxiety/panic attacks
- Sweating
- Heart palpitations
- Headache
- Concentration problems
- Muscle stiffness
- Hand tremors

More serious benzodiazepine withdrawal symptoms include:

- Hallucinations
- Seizures

- Psychosis
- Suicidal ideations

While in detox, there are numerous medications that can be used to help the body withdraw as safely as possible. Some of these medications will help ease the discomfort of withdrawal symptoms, while others can help reduce cravings. This approach is easier than going "cold turkey" and stopping drugs abruptly, which in some cases can result in seizures or even death.

Although there still may be mild discomfort during detox, medications will help make the detox as tolerable as possible. Many detox programs are staffed with qualified professionals that include: physicians, nurses, social workers, and case managers. Their job is to make sure the patients are well cared for so the detox experience is as helpful and comfortable as possible.

Detox is usually done in a hospital or outpatient clinic. The length of stay varies but is typically three to seven days. Some factors that determine if a patient is a candidate for detox include: type of drug used, if multiple drugs are used at the same time, how long an individual has been using, age, and medical history.

Although it may be medically necessary to enter into a detox program, there are some things to consider that can make the process challenging. First, three to seven days in a medically assisted program can be expensive. In many cases, health insurance will cover the cost of treatment. However, this may not be the case for everyone. Second, it is multiple days in a hospital, therefore increasing the chance of missing work, time with family, home responsibilities, and so on. Lastly, detox treatment is only to help assure a safe and comfortable detoxification of chemicals. This treatment does little to address the psychological, social, and behavioral aspects of addiction.

These concerns about detox treatment are definitely things to think about. However, the drawbacks pale in comparison to the overall benefit of being assured detoxification is safe and effective. If you or someone you know is wondering if you are a candidate for detox treatment, speak to your doctor immediately. If you do not have a doctor, you can go to the nearest hospital and visit the emergency room. Let the doctors know you have a drug dependency and need detox assistance. If they do not offer it, they should have resources for you. You can also use the resources provided at the end of this section.

Some of the benefits of detox treatment include:

- It is medically safe and supervised by professionals.
- It can minimize the pain of withdrawal.
- It can stabilize any comorbid medical conditions.
- It can handle emergency situations should they arise.
- It can administer medications to patients without hindering the detox process.
- It can maintain the patient's dignity.

Residential Treatment

Residential treatment involves living in a treatment facility. These facilities are designed for those who wish to be temporarily removed from their living situation in order to focus on recovery. Reasons a person in recovery may want or need to be away from their current living arraignments vary. Factors at home that may hinder your recovery efforts include: a person in the home who is also addicted to drugs, conflicts among those in the home, and lack of social support.

Residential treatment can be short term (thirty to ninety days) or long term (six to twelve months). Length of stay usually depends on various things such as funding, program policies, or client progress. While in the treatment facility, clients participate in a range of treatment services. These often include: individual therapy, group therapy, education sessions, and case management services. Therapy and educational experiences will help with the psychological and behavioral components of addiction. Case management services can assist patients with housing (if necessary), referrals to outpatient services, and even employment services.

Residential treatment can be expensive. Although health insurance may cover the cost of some residential treatment centers, this is not the case for all of them. Also, the location of the residential treatment center may require travel. This also can be expensive. Long stays in a residential program means time off work and time away from home and families.

If you or someone you know is looking for a residential treatment facility, consider the following tips. In a web search engine type "residential treatment" and the name of your city in the search box. If that does not provide anything useful, search for "addiction treatment" or "addiction services" and see if that helps. You can also use the resources provided at the end of this section.

Intensive Outpatient Programs (IOP)

Sometimes a person seeking an intensive treatment does not necessarily need a residential treatment program. Normally, this is because their living environment is already filled with safety, consistency, and security. In these cases, even though a new living environment is not necessary, the other benefits of intense treatment are still needed.

Intensive outpatient programs (IOP) are designed to give many of the services residential treatment provides, but in an outpatient setting. One other difference is that IOP is usually not daily but rather three days a week. It typically lasts six to twelve months but can last longer. As is true with residential treatment, length of stay depends on various factors.

The treatment services in IOP are very similar to those in residential treatment. These include: group therapy, education sessions, and case management services. In some cases, IOP may include AA or NA participation. These services will help with the psychological and behavioral components of addiction. Case management services can assist clients with referrals to other outpatient therapy services, school enrollment, and employment services, to name a few.

The cost of IOP programs vary. In some cases, medical insurance will cover IOP treatment. There are also some programs that are grant funded. The best way to find out is to locate a program and ask how treatment is paid for.

If you or someone you know is looking for an intensive outpatient program, consider these tips. In a web browser type "intensive outpatient treatment" and the name of your city in the search box. If that does not provide anything useful, search for "outpatient addiction treatment" or "addiction services" and see if that helps. You can also use the resources provided at the end of this section.

Outpatient Programs (OP)

Outpatient treatment programs are less time consuming and offer fewer treatment services than IOP programs. Ordinarily, group therapy meetings are held two, rather than three, times per week. Outpatient programs can be a step down from either residential or IOP as part of a continuing care plan. Clients are able to remain in treatment for a couple of sessions every week while freeing up time to take care of other personal responsibilities.

Since clients in OP programs are only receiving services twice a week, the cost is significantly lower than both residential and IOP treatment. In some cases, medical insurance can cover OP treatment. There are also some programs that are grant funded.

If you, or someone you know, is looking for an outpatient program, consider these tips. In a web browser type "outpatient treatment" and the name of your city in the search box. If that does not provide anything useful, search for "outpatient addiction treatment" or "addiction services" and see if that helps. You can also use the resources provided at the end of this section.

Psychotherapy

Psychotherapy is also referred to as "therapy" or "counseling." Psychotherapy is a way to help people work through a variety of issues that they either cannot or do not want to face alone. Some common problems people seek psychotherapy for are: life adjustments, grief, relational problems, mental health disorders, and addiction. Therapy sessions are typically once a week for forty-five to sixty minutes. Psychotherapy can be short term (weeks) or long term (years). The length depends on several factors including: complexity of the problem, client availability, strength of the therapeutic relationship, and cost, to name a few. There are four main types of psychotherapy: individual, couples, family, and group.

Individual Therapy

Individual therapy is probably the most popular form of psychotherapy. Individual therapy is a one-on-one, confidential relationship between a therapist and a client. During therapy sessions, both the therapist and the client work collaboratively to solve the client's problem.

Couples Therapy

Couples therapy, also referred to as "couples counseling," involves therapy in which a couple meets with a mental health professional to work through relationship issues. Often, couples counseling is directed at fixing problems in the relationship. However, couples can also seek therapy to help them learn more about one another and strengthen the relationship.

Family Therapy

Family therapy occurs when a mental health professional meets with a family unit. Sessions can include parts of a family or the entire family. Family therapy is designed to enhance familial relationships or resolve problems. The goals are specific to the family's unique situation or circumstances.

Group Therapy

In group therapy, a group of individuals meets together for psychotherapy. Group therapy is typically led by one or two mental health professionals. Members of a group often share similar problems or circumstances. The size of therapy groups varies and there is not a "right" or "wrong" number for a group. The most important thing is that a group is facilitated in a way that allows group members to express thoughts and feelings in a "safe" environment and help one another.

Finding the Right Therapist

Finding a good therapist is all about relationship chemistry. If you are comfortable with the therapist who is helping you, then it's a good fit. If you are not comfortable, you may have to "shop around" until you find someone you feel a connection with. Just keep in mind that a relationship takes time to develop. It can be very difficult to know if there is a connection after only one session. You may want to give it a few sessions before you decide if the relationship will work for you.

If you are looking for therapy of any kind, you can start by talking with your doctor. However, you can also use the Internet and search for therapists near you. Just type in "therapy" and your town or city in the search box.

Twelve-Step Groups

Dozens of twelve-step groups are available in the United States. More details about each of them may be found on the Internet.

Alcoholics Anonymous (AA) is the oldest self-help group in the nation. AA is for alcoholics who are seeking recovery. AA has a website that offers a fund of information. On it you will also find a meeting locator to search for meetings near you. Website: www.aa.org

Narcotics Anonymous (NA) is for those who are addicted to narcotics. Visit the NA website for more information. The site also includes a meeting locator to search for meetings near you. Website: www.na.org.

Other Twelve-Step Organizations

Here is a listing of twelve-step group meetings available in the United States:

- Adult Children of Alcoholics (ACA)
- Clutterers Anonymous (CLA)
- Cocaine Anonymous (CA)
- Codependents Anonymous (CoDA)
- CoSex and Love Addicts Anonymous (COSLAA)
- Crystal Meth Anonymous (CMA)
- Debtors Anonymous (DA)
- Emotions Anonymous (EA)
- Families Anonymous (FA)
- Food Addicts Anonymous (FAA)
- Food Addicts in Recovery Anonymous (FA)
- Gamblers Anonymous (GA)
- Heroin Anonymous (HA)
- Marijuana Anonymous (MA)
- Narcotics Anonymous (NA)

- Neurotics Anonymous (N/A)
- Nicotine Anonymous (NicA)
- Overeaters Anonymous (OA)
- Pills Anonymous (PA)
- Racists Anonymous (RA)
- Sex Addicts Anonymous (SAA)
- Sexaholics Anonymous (SA)
- Sex and Love Addicts Anonymous (SLAA)
- Sexual Compulsives Anonymous (SCA)
- Sexual Recovery Anonymous (SRA)
- Survivors of Incest Anonymous (SIA)
- Underearners Anonymous (UA)
- Workaholics Anonymous (WA)

Twelve-Step Groups for Family Members

If you have a family member or loved one who is suffering from addiction and you are interested in a twelve-step group, here is a listing of groups for family and loved ones:

Al-Anon

A group for family members who are dealing with an alcoholic in the family. At these meetings, families have opportunities to learn from and support one another. Al-Anon also has a website with resources including a meeting locator. Website: al-anon.org.

Codependents Anonymous

Designed to help people coping with codependency. The groups strive to help each other develop functional, healthy relationships. Website: Coda.org.

Gam-Anon

Help for family and friends of gamblers. Website: gamblersanonymous.org.

Nar-Anon

Similar to Narcotics Anonymous, Nar-Anon is for family members of those who are addicted to narcotics. In these groups, members learn from each other about coping with a narcotics addict in the family circle. Website: www.nar-anon.org.

Education Groups

Education groups are common in treatment programs. Different from therapy groups, education groups focus on learning about topics such as highway safety, internal drug triggers, and drug effects. Education groups may involve a lot of peer participation or may be structured more like a lecture or presentation. Education groups are sometimes facilitated by a licensed professional. However, unlike therapy, there is usually no special license or formal education needed to run this type of group. Common programs that use education groups are hospital detox centers, residential and outpatient programs, and court-ordered treatment programs.

Resources

Above the Influence
Above the Influence is a nonprofit organization aimed at helping teenagers stand up to peer pressure. Their website includes information on types of peer influences, drug abuse, how to get involved, and where to find help. Website: abovetheinfluence.com.

Center on Addiction
Center on Addiction is a nonprofit organization that focuses on drug prevention and recovery. Their website provides help for families who are dealing with addiction. It includes information on addiction and prevention, treatment, as well as a library of books and journals. Website: centeronaddiction.org.

The National Drug Helpline
The National Drug Helpline is an organization that helps anyone with mental health or substance use problems gain access to resources. Their website provides both phone numbers and websites to assist those in need. The National Drug Helpline is (844) 289-0879. Website: Drughelpline.org.

National Institute on Drug Abuse (NIDA)
NIDA focuses on the scientific advances that either explain the cause of addiction or improve the quality of addiction treatment. NIDA's website includes current stats and trends for drugs of abuse, current research on drugs and treatment, and various publications. Website: drugabuse.gov.

Substance Abuse and Mental Health Services (SAMHSA)

SAMHSA is connected to the U.S. Department of Health and Human Services. SAMHSA aims to reduce the consequences of substance use and mental health disorders in the United States. SAMHSA's website offers information about their organization, data on substance abuse and mental disorders, and treatment information, which includes treatment locators. SAMHSA also provides the National Helpline phone number, which provides assistance to those needing help. The National Helpline number is (800) 662-HELP (4357). Website: SAMHSA. gov.

Index

Index

healthy expression of, 68, 74
  identifying, 56, 57
  impaired ability to express,
    16
food addiction, 3
Freud, Sigmund, 25
friends and family, 9, 73, 79–86,
  89
  and the changing you, 82–84

G

Gam-Anon, 114
Gamblers Anonymous (GA), 87
gambling addiction, 3
goal setting, 40
grief, 63, 64, 111
  expressing, 63, 64
  unresolved, 63
group therapy, 36, 109, 110, 111,
  112
guided imagery, 60, 61, 62, 72

H

habit changes, 58
health insurance, 108, 109
healthy relationships
  benefits, 79, 80
healthy selfishness as a tool, 9,
  17, 18, 101
heroin, 103
hydrocodone, 103

I

"I" statements, 74
individual therapy, 109, 111
*Inner Work: Using Dreams
  and Active Imagination for
  Personal Growth,* 60
insurance, 108, 109
intensive outpatient programs
  (IOP), 110
  cost, 110
internal exercises, 54

intrusive thoughts, 58

J

Johnson, Robert A., 60
journal writing, 40, 41, 52, 55,
  56, 72
  dreams, 60
Jung, Carl, G., 24, 25

L

learned skills, 49, 50
limit setting, 68, 71, 75, 82, 86

M

manipulation, 83, 84
marijuana, 3
material wants, 48
medical-assisted therapy (MAT),
  103
medical detoxification, 106
  see also detoxification
meditation, 58, 59
mental health disorders, 111
mental illness, 4
morphine, 103
motivational interviewing, 4

N

naloxone, 104
naltrexone, 4, 104
Nar-Anon, 115
Narcan, 104, 105, 106
  usage, 105
narcissist, 48, 51, 97
Narcotics Anonymous (NA), 87,
  110, 113, 115
National Institute on Drug Abuse
  (NIDA), 5
neurons, 56
neuroreceptors, 56

O

opiates, 103
  withdrawal, 104

Index

socialization, 13
spending
    irresponsible, 21, 22
sponsor/sponsee relationships,
    91
sponsors, 91
stress, 40, 58, 60
Suboxone, 104
Substance Abuse and
    Mental Health Services
    Administration (SAMHSA), 5
support groups, 4, 8, 73
supportive relationships, 80

T

temper tantrums, 28, 43, 44, 50
    see also adult temper tantrum
    exercise
therapists, 4, 60
    finding, 112
therapy groups, 49
time for self, 52
tobacco, 3
treatment options, 103–115
troublemaking
    redefining, 65–76
troublemaking as a tool, 17, 18,
    65–76, 101
    characteristics, 65
true-self, 12, 19, 23, 26, 48, 59,
    62, 63, 68, 75, 82, 91, 93, 101
    honoring, 14
    internal division, 24
    limitation, 12
    loss, 12
    neglect, 38
    suppression, 30, 31
twelve-step programs, 2, 87, 88,
    113
    benefits, 89
    for family members, 114

W

what-self, 48, 49
window shopping exercise, 54
withdrawal symptoms, 104, 106,
    108
pain associated with, 109
World Health Organization
    (WHO), 105

About the Author

Timothy J. Wulff, L.M.S.W., A.C.S.W., is a licensed clinical social worker. He holds a clinical license through the state of Michigan and currently maintains a private practice with Comprehensive Psychological Services in East Lansing, Michigan.

For more than a decade, Mr. Wulff has been studying the neurochemical, emotional, familial, and social impact of addiction. His unique approach to treatment has helped hundreds of clients gain a deeper understanding of why they become stuck in an addictive cycle. In 2019, his article, "Recover Yourself: A Different Perspective on Addiction and Recovery," appeared in *Counselor: The Magazine for Addiction Professionals.* The article detailed his method of treatment for addictive disorders.

Mr. Wulff has also completed training in Eye Movement Desensitization and Reprocessing (EMDR) therapy in order to help clients heal from intense trauma. He graduated in 2003 with a bachelor of science degree from Grand Valley State University in Allendale, Michigan. In 2007, he received a master's degree in clinical social work from Michigan State University in East Lansing, Michigan.

Mr. Wulff resides in Grand Ledge, Michigan with his wife Kara and two children, Grayson and Gabriella. He can be reached by e-mail at: **Timothywulff@gmail.com.**

Consumer Health Titles from Addicus Books

Visit our online catalog at www.AddicusBooks.com